MICROSOFT® OFFICE
OneNote™ 2003

Introductory Concepts and Techniques

Gary B. Shelly
Thomas J. Cashman
Philip J. Pratt
Mary Z. Last

THOMSON
COURSE TECHNOLOGY™

COURSE TECHNOLOGY
25 THOMSON PLACE
BOSTON MA 02210

 SHELLY
CASHMAN
SERIES®

Australia • Canada • Denmark • Japan • Mexico • New Zealand • Philippines • Puerto Rico
Singapore • South Africa • Spain • United Kingdom • United States

Microsoft Office® OneNote™ 2003
Introductory Concepts and Techniques

Gary B. Shelly
Thomas J. Cashman
Philip J. Pratt
Mary Z. Last

Executive Director:
Cheryl Costantini

Senior Acquisitions Editor:
Dana Merk

Senior Editor:
Alexandra Arnold

Series Consulting Editor:
Jim Quasney

Product Manager:
Reed Cotter

Editorial Assistant:
Selena Coppock

Marketing Manager:
Andy Bernier

Production Editor:
Philippa Lehar

Print Buyer:
Laura Burns

Interior Designer:
Becky Herrington

Development Editor:
Ginny Harvey

Printer:
Banta Menasha

Copy Editor:
Lyn Markowicz

Proofreader:
Nancy Lamm

Compositor/Illustrator:
GEX Publishing Services

Cover Design:
Ken Russo

Cover Illustration:
Richard Herrera

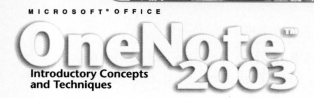

MICROSOFT® OFFICE

Introductory Concepts
and Techniques

Contents

Preface

The Shelly Cashman Series® offers the finest textbooks in computer education. We are proud of the fact that our series of Microsoft Office 4.3, Microsoft Office 95, Microsoft Office 97, Microsoft Office 2000, and Microsoft Office XP textbooks have been the most widely used books in education. With each new edition of our Office books, we have made significant improvements based on the software and comments made by the instructors and students. The *Microsoft Office 2003* books continue with the innovation, quality, and reliability that you have come to expect from the Shelly Cashman Series.

In this *Microsoft Office OneNote 2003* book, you will find an educationally sound, highly visual, and easy-to-follow pedagogy that combines a vastly improved step-by-step approach with corresponding screens. All projects and exercises in this book are designed to take full advantage of the OneNote 2003 Service Pack 1 features. The project material is developed to ensure that students will see the importance of learning OneNote 2003 for future coursework. The popular Other Ways and More About features offer in-depth knowledge of OneNote 2003. The new Q&A feature offers students a way to solidify important personal information management concepts. The Learn It Online page presents a wealth of additional exercises to ensure your students have all the reinforcement they need.

Objectives of this Textbook

Microsoft Office OneNote 2003: Introductory Concepts and Techniques is intended for a course that covers a brief introduction to OneNote 2003. No experience with a computer is assumed, and no mathematics beyond the high school freshman level is required. The objectives of this book are:

- To teach the fundamentals of OneNote 2003
- To expose students to practical examples of the computer as a useful tool
- To acquaint students with organizing and storing notes electronically
- To develop an exercise-oriented approach that allows learning by doing
- To encourage independent study and help those who are working alone

The Shelly Cashman Approach

Features of the Shelly Cashman Series *Microsoft Office OneNote 2003* books include:

- Project Orientation Each project in the book presents a practical problem and complete solution in an easy-to-understand approach.
- Step-by-Step, Screen-by-Screen Instructions Each of the tasks required to complete a project is identified throughout the project. Full-color screens accompany the steps.
- Thoroughly Tested Projects Unparalleled quality is ensured because every screen in the book is produced by the author only after performing a step, and then each project must pass Course Technology's award-winning Quality Assurance program.
- Other Ways Boxes and Quick Reference Summary The Other Ways boxes displayed at the end of most of the step-by-step sequences specify the other ways to do the task completed in the steps. Thus, the steps and the Other Ways box make a comprehensive reference unit. The Quick Reference Summary at the back of the book summarizes the ways you can complete a task using the mouse, menu, shortcut menu, and keyboard.

Other Ways

1. On File menu click New, click Folder in New task pane
2. Right-click currently selected folder or section, click New Folder on shortcut menu

■ **More About and Q&A Features** These marginal annotations provide background information, tips, and answers to common questions that complement the topics covered, adding depth and perspective to the learning process.

■ **Integration of the World Wide Web** The World Wide Web is integrated into the OneNote 2003 learning experience by (1) More About annotations that send students to Web sites for up-to-date information and alternative approaches to tasks; (2) a OneNote 2003 Quick Reference Summary Web page that summarizes the ways to complete tasks (mouse, menu, shortcut menu, and keyboard); and (3) the Learn It Online page at the end of each project, which has project reinforcement exercises, learning games, and other types of student activities.

Organization of this Textbook

Microsoft Office OneNote 2003: Introductory Concepts and Techniques provides basic instruction on how to use OneNote. The material is divided into two projects, an Integration feature, an appendix, and a Quick Reference Summary.

Project 1 – Taking Notes In Project 1, students are introduced to the concept of the notebook and shown how to use OneNote to take notes. Topics include creating, renaming, opening, closing, and deleting sections; adding a page title; adding a note container; moving a container; resizing a container; deleting a container; splitting a container; formatting and highlighting characters; adding a page; adding a list; moving items in a list; creating an outline; adding note flags; using a To Do note flag; adding pictures; adding a drawing; using handwriting; adding a subpage; and adding a table. Other topics include printing all pages in a section; printing the current page; using rule lines; performing a backup; opening a backup file; and using OneNote Help.

Project 2 – Organizing and Using Notes In Project 2, students learn to organize their notes. Topics include creating folders; moving sections; inserting new sections; moving pages; deleting pages; grouping pages; and navigating in the notebook. Other topics include using stationery when creating pages; creating numbered lists; searching notes; viewing a note flags summary; creating a Note Flags Summary page; taking side notes; viewing side notes; checking spelling; and modifying, expanding, and collapsing an outline.

Integration Feature – Integrating OneNote with Other Applications In this Integration Feature, students learn how to integrate OneNote with other applications. Topics include copying content from other applications to OneNote; copying content from OneNote to other applications; using the Research task pane; pasting a Web page to OneNote; saving sections to other locations; sharing sections with other users; using OneNote with Outlook; recording notes; playing back notes; and using typed notes to playback notes from specific locations.

Appendix – Changing Screen Resolution and Customizing OneNote This appendix shows students how to change screen resolution and how to customize OneNote in a variety of ways. Topics include changing screen resolution; resetting toolbars and menus; hiding page titles; and changing the notebook location. It also covers all the additional customizations possible by using the Options command on the Tools menu.

Quick Reference Summary In OneNote, you can accomplish a task in a number of ways, such as using the mouse, menu, shortcut menu, and keyboard. The Quick Reference Summary at the back of the book provides a quick reference to each task presented.

End-of-Project Student Activities

A notable strength of this Shelly Cashman Series *Microsoft OneNote 2003* book is the extensive student activities at the end of each project. Well-structured student activities can make the difference between students merely participating in a class and students retaining the information they learn. The activities in the Shelly Cashman Series *OneNote 2003* books include the following.

- **What You Should Know** A listing of the tasks completed within a project together with the pages on which the step-by-step, screen-by-screen explanations appear. The tasks are listed in the same order they are presented in the project.
- **Learn It Online** Every project features a Learn It Online page that comprises twelve exercises. These exercises include True/False, Multiple Choice, Short Answer, Flash Cards, Practice Test, Learning Games, Tips and Tricks, Newsgroup usage, Expanding Your Horizons, Search Sleuth, Office Online Training, and Office Marketplace.
- **Apply Your Knowledge** This exercise usually requires students to open and manipulate a file on the Data Disk that parallels the activities learned in the project. To obtain a copy of the Data Disk, follow the instructions on the inside back cover of this textbook.
- **In The Lab** Three in-depth assignments per project require students to utilize the project concepts and techniques to solve problems on a computer.
- **Cases and Places** Five unique real-world case-study situations, including one small-group activity.

Instructor Resources CD-ROM

The Shelly Cashman Series is dedicated to providing you with all of the tools you need to make your class a success. Information on all supplementary materials is available through your Course Technology representative or by calling one of the following telephone numbers: Colleges and Universities, 1-800-648-7450; High Schools, 1-800-824-5179; Private Career Colleges, 1-800-347-7707; Canada, 1-800-268-2222; Corporations with IT Training Centers, 1-800-648-7450; and Government Agencies, Health-Care Organizations, and Correctional Facilities, 1-800-477-3692.

The Instructor Resources for this textbook include both teaching and testing aids. The contents of each item on the Instructor Resources CD-ROM (ISBN 0-619-25504-8) are described on the facing page.

INSTRUCTOR'S MANUAL The Instructor's Manual is made up of Microsoft Word files, which include detailed lesson plans with page number references, lecture notes, teaching tips, classroom activities, discussion topics, projects to assign, and transparency references. The transparencies are available through the Figure Files described on the facing page.

LECTURE SUCCESS SYSTEM The Lecture Success System consists of intermediate files that correspond to certain figures in the book, allowing you to step through the creation of an application in a project during a lecture without entering large amounts of data.

SYLLABUS Sample syllabi, which can be customized easily to a course, are included. The syllabi cover policies, class and lab assignments and exams, and procedural information.

FIGURE FILES Illustrations for every figure in the textbook are available in electronic form. Use this ancillary to present a slide show in lecture or to print transparencies for use in lecture with an overhead projector. If you have a personal computer and LCD device, this ancillary can be an effective tool for presenting lectures.

POWERPOINT PRESENTATIONS PowerPoint Presentations is a multimedia lecture presentation system that provides slides for each project. Presentations are based on project objectives. Use this presentation system to present well-organized lectures that are both interesting and knowledge based. PowerPoint Presentations provides consistent coverage at schools that use multiple lecturers.

SOLUTIONS TO EXERCISES Solutions are included for the end-of-project exercises, as well as the Project Reinforcement exercises.

TEST BANK & TEST ENGINE The ExamView test bank includes 110 questions for every project (25 multiple-choice, 50 true/false, and 35 completion) with page number references, and when appropriate, figure references. A version of the test bank you can print also is included. The test bank comes with a copy of the test engine, ExamView, the ultimate tool for your objective-based testing needs. ExamView is a state-of-the-art test builder that is easy to use. ExamView enables you to create paper-, LAN-, or Web-based tests from test banks designed specifically for your Course Technology textbook. Utilize the ultra-efficient QuickTest Wizard to create tests in less than five minutes by taking advantage of Course Technology's question banks, or customize your own exams from scratch.

DATA FILES FOR STUDENTS All the files that are required by students to complete the exercises are included. You can distribute the files on the Instructor Resources CD-ROM to your students over a network, or you can have them follow the instructions on the inside back cover of this book to obtain a copy of the Data Disk.

ADDITIONAL ACTIVITIES FOR STUDENTS These additional activities consist of Project Reinforcement Exercises, which are true/false, multiple choice, and short-answer questions that help students gain confidence in the material learned.

Online Content

Course Technology offers textbook-based content for Blackboard, WebCT, and MyCourse 2.1

BLACKBOARD AND WEBCT As the leading provider of IT content for the Blackboard and WebCT platforms, Course Technology delivers rich content that enhances your textbook to give your students a unique learning experience. Course Technology has partnered with WebCT and Blackboard to deliver our market-leading content through these state-of-the-art online learning platforms.

MYCOURSE 2.1 MyCourse 2.1 is Course Technology's powerful online course management and content delivery system. Completely maintained and hosted by Thomson, MyCourse 2.1 delivers an online learning environment that is completely secure and provides superior performance. MyCourse 2.1 allows nontechnical users to create, customize, and deliver World Wide Web-based courses; post content and assignments; manage student enrollment; administer exams; track results in the online gradebook; and more.

MICROSOFT OFFICE ONENOTE

MICROSOFT
Office OneNote 2003

Taking Notes

PROJECT

1

CASE PERSPECTIVE

Alyssa Ashton is a student at Penn County Community College (PCCC). Alyssa is pursuing an Associate in Applied Science (A.A.S.) degree in Business Administration. Students who graduate from PCCC with a degree in Business Administration qualify for entry-level positions in many areas of business. Students also may transfer to a four-year college and apply the degree toward a Bachelor of Science degree in Business Administration.

Alyssa is pursuing a degree in Business Administration because she wants to gain the knowledge necessary to manage her own business. Alyssa has a talent for arts and crafts. Currently, Alyssa is making hand-painted glassware, such as soap dispensers, salt and pepper shakers, and candle holders. She sells her glassware at area craft fairs and festivals.

Similar to many other community college students, Alyssa juggles multiple priorities. In addition to her studies at the community college, Alyssa is taking a pottery-making class at the community art association. She also volunteers at the local animal shelter.

Last semester, Alyssa noticed several of her classmates using Microsoft OneNote on a Tablet PC. A Tablet PC is a lightweight version of a PC in the shape of a flat panel. Users can enter data using the keyboard. They also can use a pen-like device to handwrite notes on the screen. Students who used the Microsoft OneNote software could take notes (Figure 1-1), organize the notes, search the notes, print them, and send them as e-mail attachments. Alyssa wants to learn to use OneNote to help her in her marketing class this semester. She is particularly interested in using OneNote for this class because it requires a team project. She hopes that OneNote will be useful both for taking notes and for managing the team project.

As you read through this project, you will learn how to use OneNote for note-taking.

Taking Notes

Objectives

You will have mastered the material in this project when you can:

- Start and customize OneNote
- Manipulate sections
- Add page titles
- Work with containers
- Format and highlight characters
- Create lists and outlines
- Add and use note flags

- Add pictures
- Use drawing and handwriting
- Add subpages and tables
- Print pages and specify print options
- Understand the backup process
- Use the OneNote Help system to answer questions

OneNote 2003 Service Pack 1

If you are stepping through the projects in this book on a computer and you want your screen to appear the same as the figures, then you must have OneNote 2003 Service Pack 1 installed. You can verify if you already have OneNote 2003 Service Pack 1 installed by following these steps: (1) start OneNote; (2) click Help on the menu bar; and (3) click About Microsoft Office OneNote on the Help menu. If SP1 appears at the end of the first line of text at the top of the About Microsoft Office OneNote dialog box, then OneNote 2003 Service Pack 1 is installed on your computer.

What Is Microsoft Office OneNote 2003?

Microsoft Office OneNote 2003 is a note-taking program. It assists you in entering, saving, organizing, searching, and using your notes. It enables you to create pages, which are organized in sections, just as in a physical notebook. In OneNote, you can type notes anywhere on a page and then easily move the notes around on the page. You can create lists and outlines. You can use handwriting to enter notes, and you also can create drawings. Although you can enter handwriting in any environment, if you do it from a Tablet PC, OneNote can convert your handwriting to text as well as search your handwriting. You can incorporate pictures as well as data from other applications in your notes.

You can take audio notes. For example, you could record what is said at a meeting or in lecture. As you record, you can take additional notes. When you play the audio notes, you can have your additional notes synchronized; that is, OneNote will show you during playback exactly the points at which you took these additional notes.

You can flag notes as being important by using a variety of note flags, which are special symbols that call your attention to important notes on a page. You then can view the specific notes that you flagged in this fashion using the Note Flags summary, which can be ordered in a variety of ways.

You can organize your notebook in whatever way is most convenient for you. OneNote includes tools to make it easy to organize your notebook and to navigate through your notebook. It also includes a search facility to make it easy to find the specific notes in which you are interested. For short notes that you always want to have readily available, you can use Side Notes. Side Notes are similar to Post-it notes that you might use in a physical notebook.

OneNote is integrated with Microsoft Office 2003 and Windows SharePoint Services, making it easy to share your notes with others.

Project One — Taking Notes

To illustrate the process of taking notes using OneNote, this book presents projects that use OneNote to take notes, organize notes, and use notes. Just as in a physical notebook, notes in OneNote appear on pages. These pages are organized into sec-

tions. Figure 1-1 shows a notebook with two sections, titled General and Meetings. Each section has a tab that you can use to select the section. These tabs, which appear at the top of the notebook, correspond to section tabs in a physical notebook.

The General section, which currently is selected, contains two pages. The pages have titles and tabs. The tabs appear on the right-hand side of the notebook. Just as with sections, you can use these page tabs to select pages. The page titled Course Notes is selected in the figure, as its tab indicates.

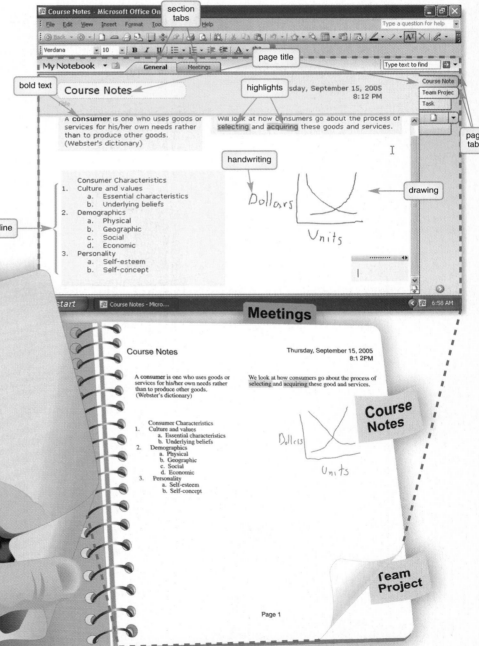

FIGURE 1-1

The Course Notes page illustrates several features of OneNote. You can format text as illustrated by the bold word, consumer. You also can format paragraphs and highlight text. In the next note, two words — selecting and acquiring — have been highlighted in yellow to draw your attention when you review these notes. The page includes an outline, which is easy to create in OneNote. If you are taking notes and your instructor sketches some type of drawing on the board, it is easy to sketch the same drawing in your notes. You also can take handwritten notes as shown in the figure.

Figure 1-2a shows the other page created in this project. The title of the page is Team Project. This page includes note flags to call your attention to important notes.

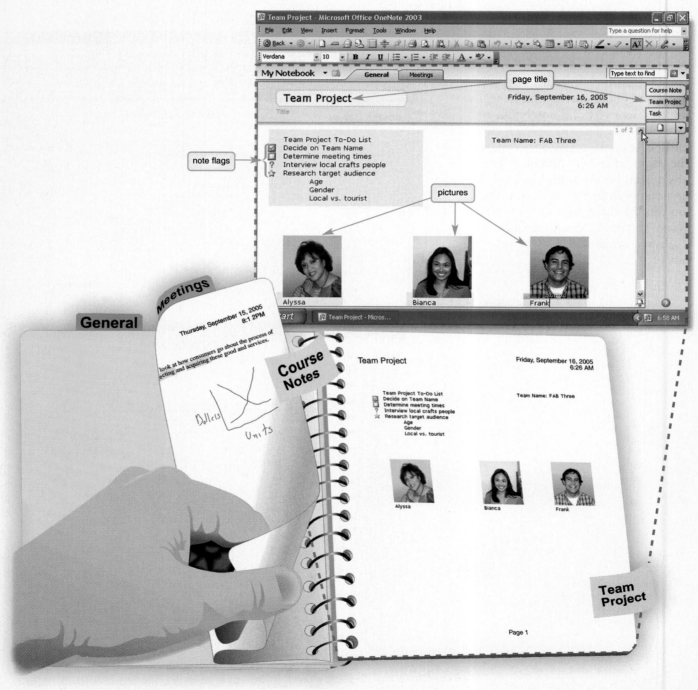

FIGURE 1-2a

Different types of note flags are available. The page in the figure also includes pictures that easily can be incorporated into your notes, as can data from Web pages and other sources.

The page in Figure 1-2a has a subpage, another page that is associated with the page in the figure. The subpage is shown in Figure 1-2b. It does not have its own title, but rather shares the title of the original page. The subpage contains a table listing the responsibilities of the team and the members who are responsible.

This project creates these notes. It shows how to navigate through the notebook as well as how to search your notes in a variety of ways. The next project shows how to organize and modify your notes.

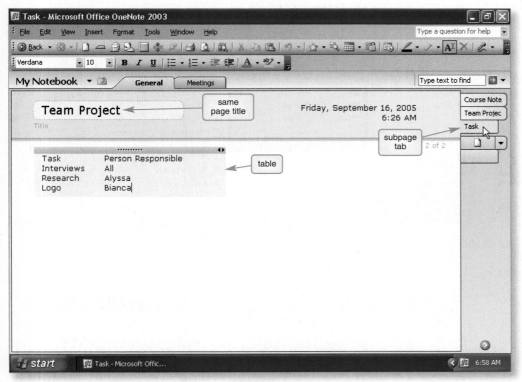

FIGURE 1-2b

Starting and Customizing OneNote

If you are stepping through this project on a computer and you want your screen to match the figures in this book, then you should change your computer's resolution to 800 × 600. For more information on how to change the resolution on your computer, see the Appendix.

The steps on the next page show how to start OneNote.

More About

OneNote and Tablet PCs

OneNote is designed to work with Tablet PCs. For more information, visit the OneNote 2003 More About Web page (scsite.com/one2003/more) and click Tablet PC.

To Start OneNote

1

• **Click the Start button on the Windows taskbar, point to All Programs on the Start menu, and then point to Microsoft Office on the All Programs submenu.**

Windows displays the Start menu, the All Programs submenu, and the Microsoft Office submenu (Figure 1-3).

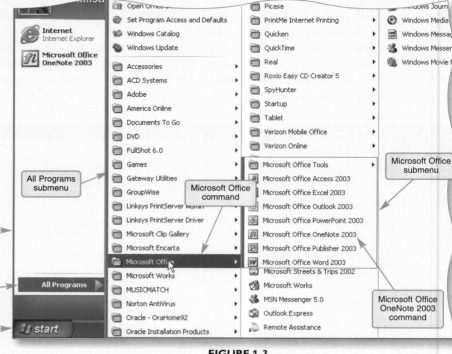

FIGURE 1-3

2

• **Click Microsoft Office OneNote 2003.**

OneNote starts. After several seconds, OneNote displays the notebook (Figure 1-4). Your screen colors might be different.

FIGURE 1-4

Other Ways

1. Double-click Microsoft Office OneNote 2003 icon on desktop
2. On Start menu click Microsoft Office OneNote 2003

Note: If you are instructed to use a special location for your notebook (for example, on a floppy disk in drive A), you need to perform the following steps as soon as you have started OneNote:
1. Click Tools on the menu bar, and then click Options on the Tools menu.
2. Click Open and Save in the Category list in the Options dialog box.
3. Click My Notebook in the Paths area and then click the Modify button.
4. When OneNote displays the Select Folder dialog box, select the folder where the notebook is located, select the folder where the notebook is located, click the Select button, and then click the OK button in the Options dialog box. Click the OK button in the Microsoft Office OneNote dialog box.
5. Quit OneNote and then restart OneNote.

For details on the above steps, see the section on Notebook location in the Appendix.

The screen in Figure 1-4 shows how the OneNote window looks the first time you start OneNote after installation on most computers. At startup, OneNote also may display a task pane on the right side of the screen. A **task pane** is a separate window that enables users to carry out some OneNote tasks more efficiently. When you start OneNote, it displays the **OneNote Help task pane**, which is a small window that you can use to obtain help on the various features of OneNote. In this book, the task pane is closed to allow the maximum width for the notebook.

At startup, OneNote displays two toolbars on a single row. To allow for more efficient use of the buttons, the toolbars should appear on two separate rows, instead of sharing a single row. The following steps show how to close the task pane and instruct OneNote to display the toolbars on two separate rows.

To Customize the OneNote Window

1

• **If the OneNote Help task pane appears in the OneNote window, click its Close button in the upper-right corner of the task pane.**

OneNote closes the OneNote Help task pane and expands the notebook to occupy the entire width of the screen (Figure 1-5).

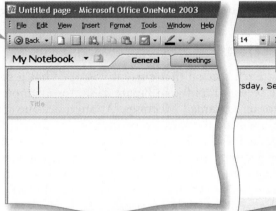
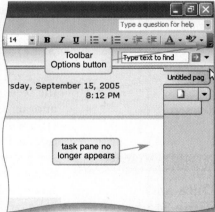

FIGURE 1-5

2

• **If the toolbars are positioned on the same row, click the Toolbar Options button.**

OneNote displays the Toolbar Options list showing the buttons that do not fit on the toolbars when toolbars appear on one row (Figure 1-6). Your toolbars may appear differently from those shown in Figure 1-6.

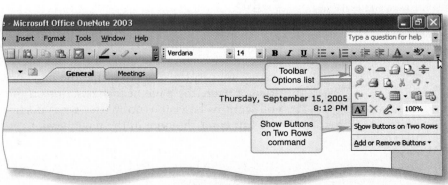

FIGURE 1-6

3

• **Click Show Buttons on Two Rows.**

OneNote displays the toolbars on two separate rows (Figure 1-7).

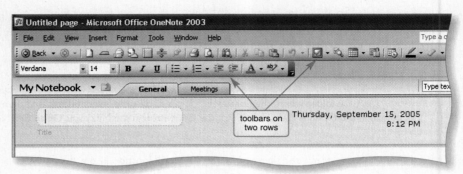

FIGURE 1-7

With the toolbars on two separate rows, all of the buttons fit on the two toolbars.

The OneNote Notebook

All activity in OneNote takes place in the **notebook** (Figure 1-8a). Like a physical notebook, the OneNote notebook consists of notes that are placed on **pages**. The pages are grouped into **sections**. Sections can be further grouped into **folders**. (No folders are shown in the notebook in the figure.)

You can use the Find box and Find button to search for specific text in your notes. You can use the Hide Page Titles button to turn off the page titles in the tabs on the right. If you click the button, the tabs will contain simply numbers and the button name will change to Show Page Titles. If you click the button a second time, the tabs once again will contain the page titles.

Sections

Each section that currently is open has a **section tab** that can be used to locate the section rapidly. In Figure 1-8a, for example, one section is named General and another is named Meetings. At anytime, one section will be the **current** section; that is, it will be the selected section. In the figure, the General section is the current section as indicated by the fact that its tab is in front of the Meetings tab.

Sections are stored as files on disk. Each section is stored as a single file whose name is the same as the section and whose extension is ONE. Thus, the General section is stored in a file named General.ONE. The file contains all the pages and subpages within the section.

Pages

Each page consists of a page area and a page header. The **page area** is the place where you typically enter your notes. The **page header** contains the **title area**, a space in which you can enter a title for the page. It also contains the **date and time stamp**, that is, the date and time the page originally was created. When you scroll down a page, the page header remains on the screen. If you have a special note that you want to be visible no matter what portion of the page currently is on the screen, you can enter the note in the page header.

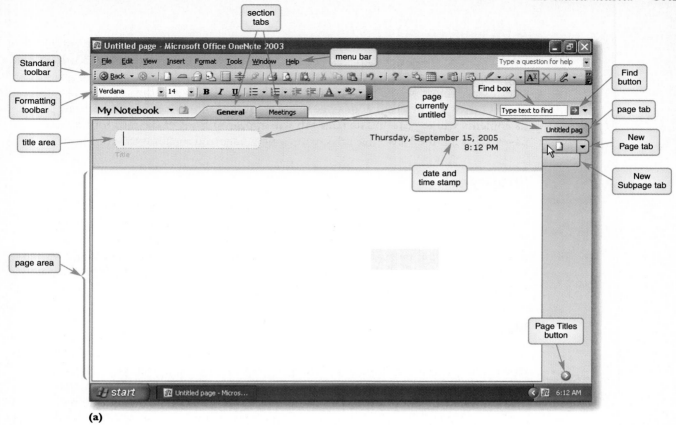

(a)

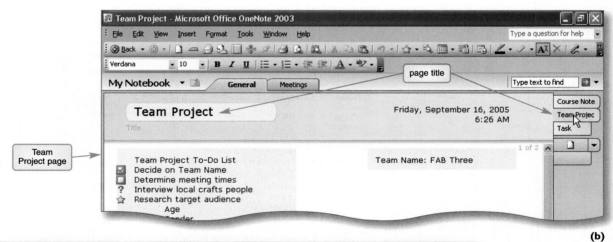

(b)

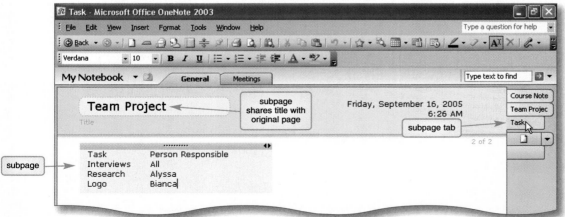

(c)

FIGURE 1-8

Each page has a **page tab** containing the title of the page if one has been entered. In Figure 1-8a on the previous page, the page is new and does not yet contain a title, so the page tab contains the words, Untitled page. In Figure 1-8b, the page has been given a title, Team Project, so the title appears in both the title area and the tab. You can move quickly to a page by clicking its page tab. The page then will become the current page. Its contents will appear and its page tab will appear in front of the tabs for the other pages. Clicking the New Page tab creates a new page and makes it the current page.

Subpages

Subpages are pages that are grouped with a specific page. Subpages do not have titles of their own. Figure 1-8c on the previous page, for example, shows a subpage that is grouped with the Team Project page. The title area contains Team Project, the title of the original page. The subpage tab contains the first bit of text entered on the subpage. A page and all its subpages form a **page group**. Clicking the New Subpage tab creates a new subpage for the current page.

Menu Bar

The **menu bar** is a special toolbar that includes the menu names (Figure 1-9a). Each **menu name** represents a menu. A **menu** is a list of commands that you can use to accomplish a variety of tasks. When you point to a menu name on the menu bar, the area of the menu bar containing the name changes to a button. To display a menu, such as the Edit menu, click the Edit menu name on the menu bar (Figure 1-9b). If you point to a menu command with an arrow to its right, OneNote displays a **submenu** from which you can choose a command.

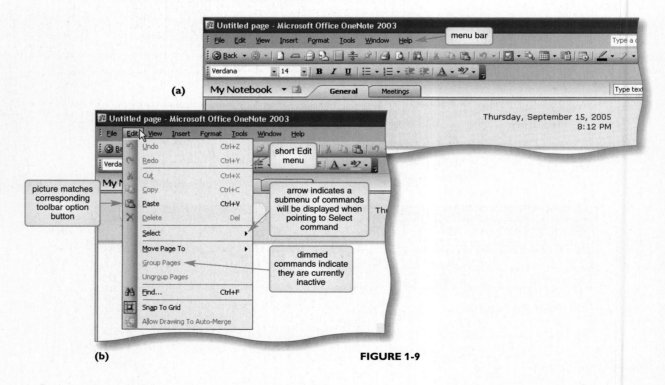

FIGURE 1-9

When you click a menu name on the menu bar, OneNote lists the commands associated with a menu (Figure 1-9b). A menu can contain some dimmed commands. A **dimmed command** appears gray, or dimmed, instead of black, which indicates it is not available for the current selection.

Standard Toolbar and Formatting Toolbar

The Standard toolbar and the Formatting toolbar (Figures 1-10a and 1-10b) contain buttons and boxes that allow you to perform frequent tasks more quickly than when using the menu bar. For example, to print a page or to print all the pages in a section, you click the Print button on the Standard toolbar. Each button has a picture on the button face to help you remember the button's function. Also, when you move the mouse pointer over a button or box, OneNote displays the name of the button or box below it in a **ScreenTip**.

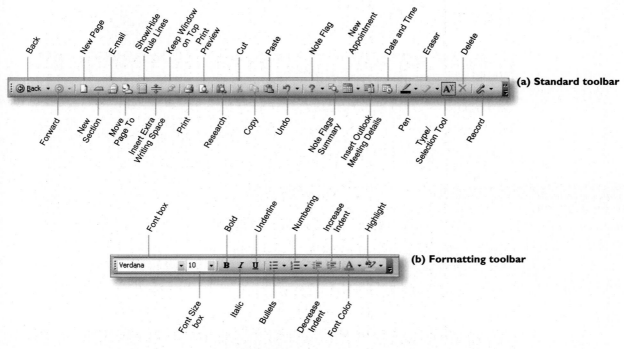

(a) Standard toolbar

(b) Formatting toolbar

FIGURE 1-10

Figures 1-10a and 1-10b illustrate the Standard and Formatting toolbars and describe the functions of the buttons. Each of the buttons and boxes will be explained in detail when they are used. The buttons that appear on your toolbar may be slightly different. For example, you may have a Redo button. You can customize the buttons that appear by clicking the Toolbar Options button, clicking the Add or Remove Buttons command, and then clicking the bytton you wish to add or remove (Figure 1-11b).

When you first install OneNote, both the Standard and Formatting toolbars are preset to appear on the same row (Figure 1-11a), immediately below the menu bar. Unless the resolution of your display device is greater than 800×600, many of the buttons that belong on these toolbars are hidden. Hidden buttons appear in the Toolbar Options list (Figure 1-11b). In this mode, you also can display all the buttons on either toolbar by double-clicking the **move handle** on the left of each toolbar (Figure 1-11a).

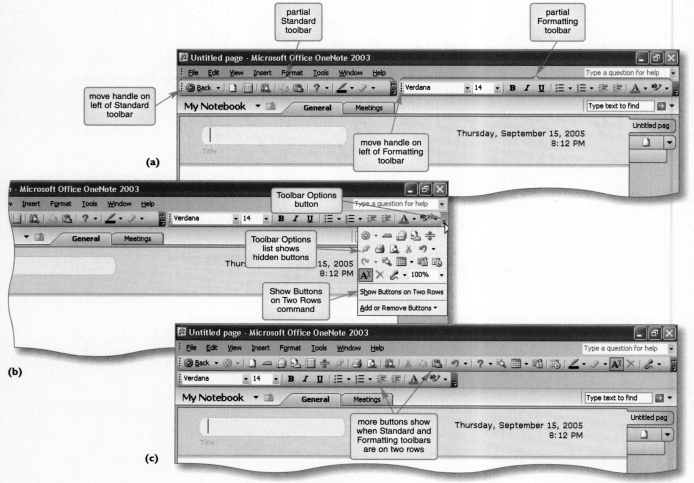

FIGURE 1-11

In this book, the Standard and Formatting toolbars are shown on two rows, one below the other, so that the buttons appear on a screen with the resolution set to 800×600 (Figure 1-11c). You can show the Standard and Formatting toolbars on two rows by using the Show Buttons on Two Rows command in the Toolbar Options list as illustrated in Figure 1-11b and described in the steps to customize the OneNote window on page ONE 9.

Sections

Typically, your initial notebook will contain two sections and, consequently, two section tabs. The two sections are titled General and Meetings. Throughout this project, you will use only the General section. As long as you have a tab for a section titled General, it does not matter what other section tabs appear in your notebook. If you have a tab that reads General, you do not need to take any further action before completing the steps in this project. You can skip to the material on adding a page title on page ONE 18. Whenever you find that you need to work with sections, you can return to the material on pages ONE 15 through ONE 18.

If you do not have a General section, you will need to add one. If you have other section tabs in addition to General and Meetings and would rather not see them, you can remove them by closing or deleting the corresponding section. (Closing removes the tab from the screen, but leaves the file for the section on disk, so you can use it in the future. Deleting removes the tab from the screen and also removes the file for the section from the disk.)

The following dicussion describes how you can manipulate these sections, should you choose to do so.

Working with Existing Sections

To close, delete, or rename a section, you first select the section by clicking its tab. Then, using the File menu and the Current Section command to produce the Current Section submenu (Figure 1-12), you can select the appropriate command from the submenu.

Closing a Section

If you no longer want a section's tab to appear, but you still want the file for the section to remain on disk, you should close the section. The following steps illustrate how to close a section.

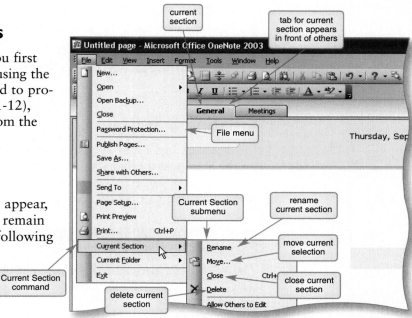

FIGURE 1-12

To Close a Section

1. Click the tab for section to be closed to make sure the section is selected.
2. Click File on the menu bar and then point to Current Section.
3. Click Close on the Current Section submenu.

The section is closed. The tab for the section no longer appears, but the file for the section still exists on disk.

Other Ways

1. Right-click section tab, click Close on shortcut menu
2. Select section, press CTRL+W

Deleting a Section

If you want the tab for a section removed from the screen and the file for the section removed from the disk, you delete the section. The steps on the next page describe how to delete a section.

Other Ways

1. Right-click section tab, click Delete on shortcut menu

TO DELETE A SECTION

1. Click the tab for the section to be deleted to make sure the section is selected.
2. Click File on the menu bar and then point to Current Section.
3. Click Delete on the Current Section submenu.
4. Click the Yes button in the Microsoft Office OneNote dialog box.

The section is deleted. The tab for the section no longer appears, and the file for the section no longer exists on disk.

Renaming a Section

To change the name of a section, you will rename the section. The following steps show how to rename a section.

Other Ways

1. Right-click section tab, click Rename on shortcut menu

TO RENAME A SECTION

1. Click the tab for the section to be renamed to make sure the section is selected.
2. Click File on the menu bar and then point to Current Section.
3. Click Rename on the Current Section submenu.
4. Type the new name for the section in the section tab and then press the ENTER key.

The name for the section is changed. The tab for the section reflects the new name.

Creating a Section

You can add a new section to your notebook by using the New Section button on the Standard toolbar (Figure 1-13). When you do, OneNote will create a new section. You then can type whatever name you want for the section. The following steps show how to create a new section.

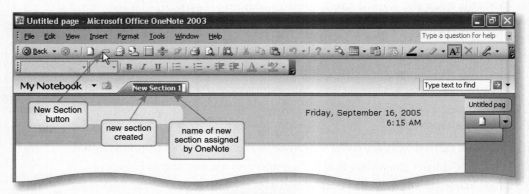

FIGURE 1-13

Other Ways

1. On File menu click New, click Section in New task pane
2. On Insert menu click New Section

TO CREATE A SECTION

1. Click the New Section button on the Standard toolbar.
2. Type the desired name for the section in the section tab.

The section now has been created. A tab with the name of the section appears in the notebook and a file for the section exists on the disk.

Opening a Section

If the file for a section already exists, but no tab for the section appears, the section is closed. To work with the section, it must be open, in which case its tab will appear. To open a section, you can use the Open command on the File menu (Figure 1-14).

After you select the Open command, you will see the File Open dialog box (Figure 1-15). You use this dialog box to select the section to be opened. The following steps illustrate how to open a section.

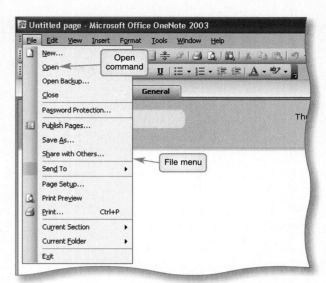

FIGURE 1-14

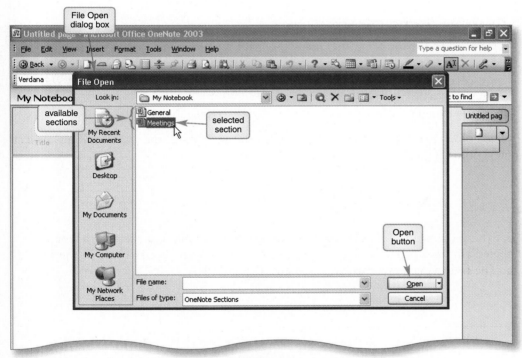

FIGURE 1-15

TO OPEN A SECTION

1. Click File on the menu bar, point to Open, and then click File on the Open submenu.
2. Navigate to the folder containing the section to be opened.
3. Select the section to be opened in the File Open dialog box, and then click the Open button.

The section is open. A tab for the section appears with the other section tabs.

Other Ways

1. Press CTRL+O

Changing a Section Color

OneNote automatically assigns colors to sections. If you would prefer to assign your own colors, you can do so by using the Section Color command on the Format menu (see Figure 1-16). The steps on the next page illustrate how to change a section color.

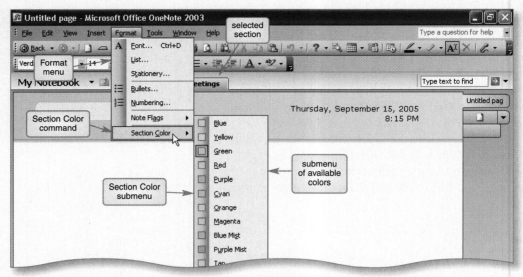

FIGURE 1-16

1. Right-click section tab, point to Section Color on shortcut menu

TO CHANGE A SECTION COLOR

1. Click the tab for the section whose color you wish to change to make sure the section is selected.
2. Click Format on the menu bar and then point to Section Color to display the submenu of available colors.
3. Click the desired color.

The color of the section is changed. The section tab and the page headings reflect the new color.

Adding a Page Title

Initially, a page is untitled; that is, its title area is left blank and the tab for the page is labeled Untitled page. A page title is added by typing the desired title in the title area. The following steps show how to add a page title.

To Add a Page Title

1

• **Click the tab for the General section if it is not already selected.**

• **If the insertion point is not positioned in the title area, click the title area to position the insertion point.**

The General section is selected (Figure 1-17). An insertion point appears in the title area.

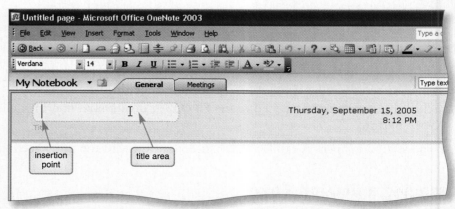

FIGURE 1-17

2

• **Type** Course Notes **in the title area of the page.**

The page title is added (Figure 1-18).

FIGURE 1-18

The title appears in both the title area of the page and in the page tab for the page.

Using Containers

In OneNote, you can add notes wherever you like on the page. When you click the position where you want to add the note and begin typing, OneNote will create a small window called a **container** that contains the note. Containers resize automatically as you enter the note. You later can move and further resize these containers.

Adding a Note and Container to a Blank Page

To add a note to a blank page, click anywhere on the page and then type the note. OneNote will create a container for the note automatically. The following step adds a note to a blank page.

To Add a Note and Container to a Blank Page

1

• **Click anywhere on the page, and then type** A consumer is one who uses goods or services for his/her own needs rather than to produce other goods. (Webster's dictionary) **as the note.**

The note is added (Figure 1-19). Yours might look slightly different depending on where you clicked on the page.

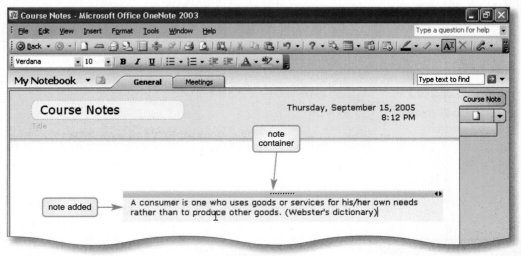

FIGURE 1-19

After the container has been added, you easily can move it. You also can resize the container.

Moving a Container

You move a container by dragging it to the new location. In order to do so, you first need to point to the bar at the top of the container until the mouse pointer shape changes to a double two-headed arrow, indicating that it can be moved. You then can drag the container. **Drag** means to point to the item, hold down the left mouse button, move the mouse pointer to the new location, then release the left mouse button. The following steps show how to move the container to the correct location.

To Move a Container

1

• **Point to the bar at the top of the container so that the mouse pointer changes to a double two-headed arrow.**

• **Drag the container to the approximate position shown in Figure 1-20. Do not release the mouse button.**

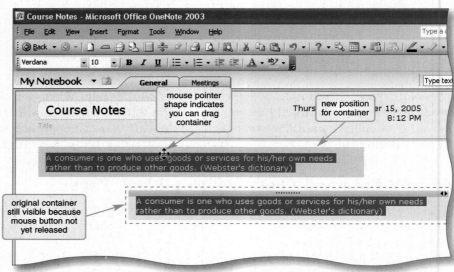

FIGURE 1-20

2

• **Release the left mouse button.**

The container is moved (Figure 1-21).

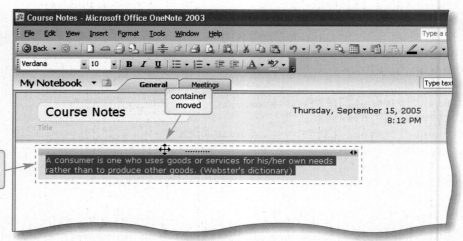

FIGURE 1-21

Other Ways

1. Right-click container, click Move on shortcut menu

With only one container on the page, it is no problem to move the container. When you have additional containers, you need to be careful not to move one container too close to another. If you do, the two containers will merge into a single container.

Using Undo

If you make a change that you realize immediately is an error, you can undo the change by selecting Edit on the menu bar and then selecting Undo on the Edit menu. This will reverse the change. The command will indicate the type of change that will be undone. For example, if you have just been typing some text, the command will read Undo Typing. If you have just moved a container, the command will read Undo Move Object. In any case, after you select Undo, the change will be reversed. You can reverse several changes, by repeatedly selecting the Undo command. You also can undo changes by clicking the Undo button on the Standard toolbar.

Resizing a Container

The container in Figure 1-21 currently is selected, as indicated by the dashed border that surrounds the container. To resize the selected container, you can point to the right border or to the left/right arrow button in the upper-right corner of the container. In either case, the mouse pointer will change to a two-headed arrow. You then can drag the pointer to resize the container. If the container is not already selected, you can click the top edge of the container to select it. The following steps resize the container, which already is selected.

To Resize a Container

1

• **Point to the right edge of the container so that the mouse pointer turns into a double two-headed arrow (Figure 1-22).**

Q&A

Q: If I undo an action accidentally, can I redo the action?

A: Yes. To redo an action that you have just undone, click Edit on the menu bar and then click Redo on the Edit menu.

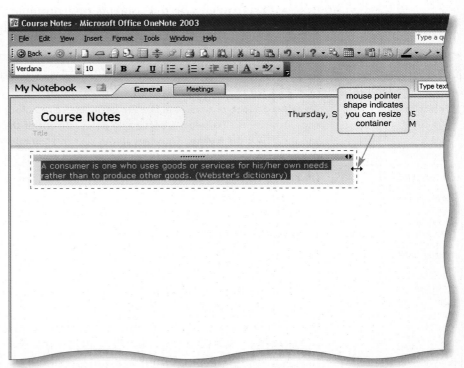

FIGURE 1-22

2

• **Drag the pointer to the position shown in Figure 1-23.**

The container is resized.

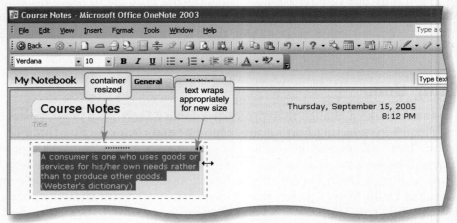

FIGURE 1-23

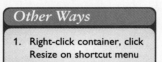

Other Ways

1. Right-click container, click Resize on shortcut menu

When you resize a container, the text will wrap appropriately for the new size.

Making Changes

Whether you have made an error when entering your notes or simply want to change what you have entered, it is easy to make changes. You can update the contents, you can delete the entire container, or you can split the contents of a container into two containers.

Updating the Contents of a Container

You can change the contents of a container. Table 1-1 indicates the various changes that are possible and the steps required to make such a change.

Table 1-1 Container Updates	
TYPE OF UPDATE	PROCESS
Select text	To select a block of text, point to the beginning of the block and then drag the mouse pointer to the end of the block. To select a paragraph, point in front of the paragraph to display a paragraph handle and then click the handle. To select all the text in a container, point to the bar at the top of the container so that the mouse pointer changes to a double two-headed arrow and then click the bar.
Insert text	Click the position for the new text, and then type the text.
Delete letter	Click immediately before the letter and then press the DELETE key. Alternatively, click immediately after the letter and then press the BACKSPACE key.
Delete block of text	Select block to be deleted and then press the DELETE key.
Copy text	Select the text to be copied and then do one of the following: click the Copy button on the Standard toolbar, click Copy on the Edit menu, or press CTRL+C.
Cut text	Select the text to be cut and then do one of the following: click the Cut button on the Standard toolbar, click Cut on the Edit menu, or press CTRL+X.
Paste text	Click the position where you want to paste the text and then do one of the following: click the Paste button on the Standard toolbar, click Paste on the Edit menu, or press CTRL+V.
Move text	Select the text to be moved and then drag it to the new location. If the location is outside the container in which the text had been located, OneNote will create a new container for the text.

Deleting a Container

You can delete a container you no longer want as shown in the following steps.

To Delete a Container

1. Click the top edge of the container to select the container.
2. Press the DELETE key.

The container will be removed from the page.

Other Ways

1. Right-click container, click Delete on shortcut menu

Splitting a Container

It is easy to inadvertently combine containers by moving one too close to another. If you discover the problem before you have taken any additional action, you can correct it by selecting Undo on the Edit menu. If not, you can split the container as shown in the following steps.

To Split a Container

1. Select the portion to be moved to a different container by dragging through it.
2. Point anywhere in the selected portion, drag the pointer to the location for the new container, and then release the left mouse button.

The selected text now will be in a separate container. You then can move or resize this container as desired.

More About

Inserting Symbols and Special Characters

You can insert symbols and other special characters in your notes. To do so, click Insert on the menu bar, click Symbol on the Insert menu. When the Symbol dialog box appears, click the desired symbol, click the Insert button, and then click the Close button.

Adding Additional Notes

The process of adding additional notes is the same as adding the original note with one exception. If you click too close to an existing container, OneNote assumes you are adding to the note in the existing container rather than adding a new one. If this happens, the insertion point will appear in a gray rectangle containing the other note. To correct this, click further away from the existing note. The following steps illustrate how to add an additional note.

To Add an Additional Note

1

• **Click away from the existing container to create a new container.**

• **Type** Will look at how consumers go about the process of selecting and acquiring these goods and services. **in the container.**

• **Move the container to the position shown in Figure 1-24 and size it to match approximately the one shown in the figure.**

The note is added to the page.

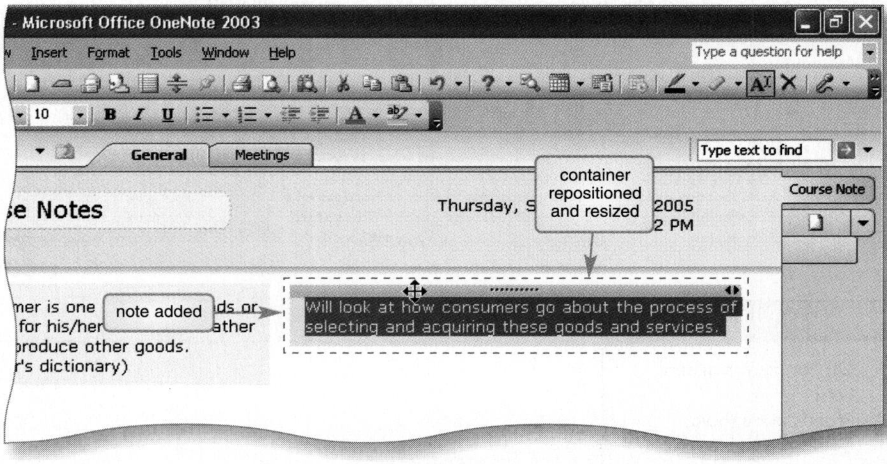

FIGURE 1-24

The second note now has been positioned and sized appropriately.

Formatting and Highlighting Characters

Just as in word processing, you can format characters in a variety of ways. You can change fonts and font sizes as well as use bold, italic, and underlining. You also can use a highlighter to highlight text, just as you would in a physical notebook.

The first note is a definition of the word, consumer. In definitions, the word being defined often appears in bold. The following steps change the word, consumer, to bold.

To Format Characters

1

• **Drag through the word, consumer, to select it.**

The word, consumer, is selected (Figure 1-25).

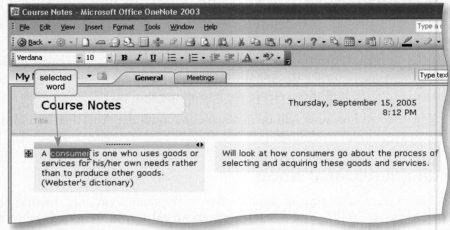

FIGURE 1-25

2

• **Click the Bold button on the Formatting toolbar.**

The word, consumer, now is bold (Figure 1-26). The word still is selected, because you have not yet clicked anywhere else on the page. The Bold button is selected. A ScreenTip for the Bold button appears, because the pointer still points to the Bold button.

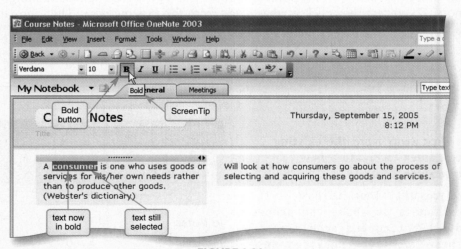

FIGURE 1-26

Other Ways

1. On Format menu click Font
2. Press CTRL+B (bold), CTRL+I (italic), or CTRL+U (underline)

In the second note, two words are important terms to remember when studying from these notes — selecting and acquiring. To help emphasize these words, you can highlight them. Highlighters are available via the Pen button on the Standard toolbar. Once you have finished highlighting, you turn the highlighter off by using the Type/Selection Tool button on the same toolbar. The following steps use a yellow highlighter to highlight the two words.

To Highlight Characters

1

• **Click the Pen button arrow on the Standard toolbar.**

The list of available pens and highlighters appears (Figure 1-27).

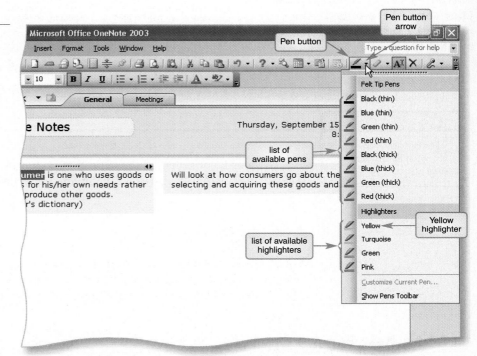

FIGURE 1-27

2

• **Click Yellow.**

• **Drag through the word, selecting, to highlight it.**

The word, selecting, is highlighted in yellow (Figure 1-28).

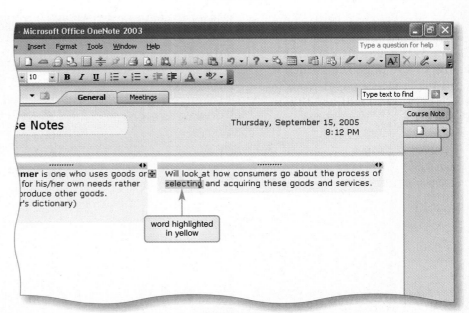

FIGURE 1-28

3

• Drag through the word, acquiring, in the second note. (If this does not highlight the word in yellow, you will need to click the Pen button another time and then drag through the word.)

• Click the Type/Selection Tool button on the Standard toolbar. Click somewhere outside the rectangle containing the highlighted words.

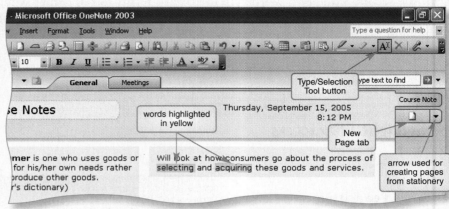

FIGURE 1-29

The word, acquiring, is highlighted in yellow (Figure 1-29). The Type/Selection Tool button is selected.

Other Ways

1. Click Highlight button arrow on Formatting toolbar

The word, consumer, in the definition now is bold, as it should be. The words, selecting and acquiring, now are highlighted in yellow to help when studying these notes.

Adding a New Page

You can add new pages to the current section at any time by using the New Page tab. The page will be untitled initially, but you can assign it a title whenever you want. The following steps show how to create a new page and then give the page a title.

To Add a New Page

1

• Click the New Page tab (see Figure 1-29). Do not click the arrow in the page tab, which is used for creating pages from stationery. (You will use this in Project 2.)

A new page is created (Figure 1-30). An insertion point appears in the title area.

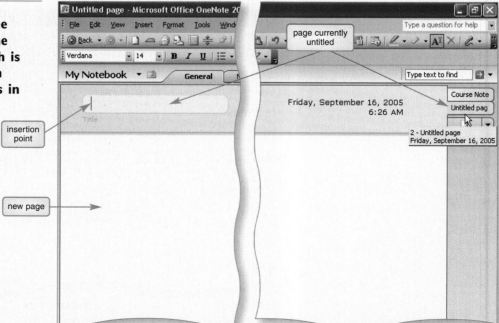

FIGURE 1-30

2

• **Type** Team Project **as the title.**

The title is entered (Figure 1-31).

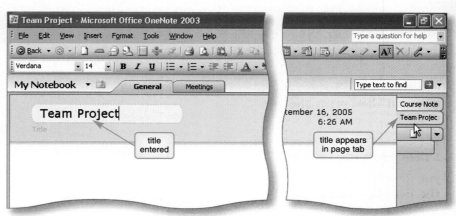

FIGURE 1-31

The title appears in both the title area and the page tab. If you inadvertently add a page you do not want, right-click the page tab and click Delete on the shortcut menu.

Other Ways

1. Click New Page button on Standard toolbar
2. On File menu click New, click New page in New task pane
3. On Insert menu click New Page
4. Right-click any page tab, click New Page on shortcut menu

Using Lists and Outlines

Notes often involve lists and outlines. OneNote makes it easy to create and update both.

Adding a List

To add a list, type the list in a container. After you finish typing an item in the list, press the ENTER key before typing the next item. Thus, each item in the list is a separate paragraph. The following steps show how to add a list to the Team Project page.

To Add a List

1

• **Click near the upper-left corner of the page and then type** Team Project To-Do List **in the container.**

A new container appears (Figure 1-32).

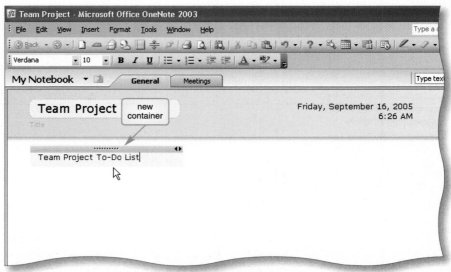

FIGURE 1-32

2

• **Press the ENTER key, type** Decide on Team Name **and then press the ENTER key.**

• **Type** Interview local crafts people **and then press the ENTER key.**

• **Type** Determine meeting times **and then press the ENTER key.**

• **Type** Research target audience **as the next line in the list.**

The list is entered (Figure 1-33).

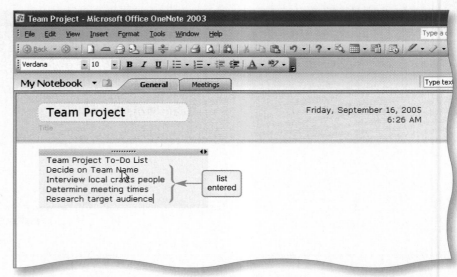

FIGURE 1-33

3

• **Press the ENTER key, press the TAB key, type** Age **as the first subcategory for Research target audience, and then press the ENTER key.**

• **Type** Gender **as the second category and then press the ENTER key.**

• **Type** Local vs. tourist **as the third category.**

The categories below Research target audience are entered (Figure 1-34).

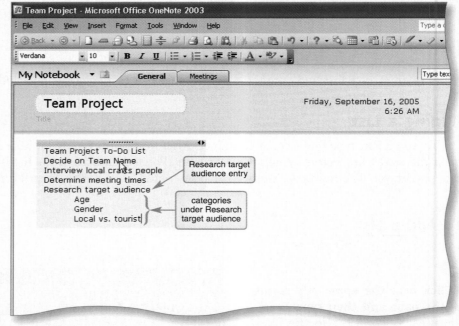

FIGURE 1-34

The list now is complete.

Changing a List

Sometimes after entering items in a list, you find that you would prefer them to be in a different order. When you point to an item in the list, a **paragraph handle** will appear to the left of the item. By dragging that handle up or down, you can move the item to a different position in the list. The following steps illustrate how to move the Determine meeting times entry one position higher in the list.

To Move Items in a List

1

• **Move the mouse pointer somewhere over the Determine meeting times entry until the paragraph handle appears.**

A paragraph handle appears to the left of the Determine meeting times entry (Figure 1-35).

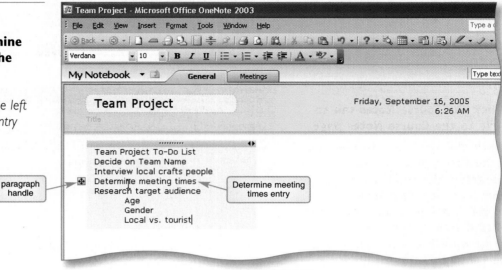

FIGURE 1-35

2

• **Drag the paragraph handle up so that the Determine meeting times entry is above the Interview local crafts people entry.**

The order of the items in the list is changed (Figure 1-36).

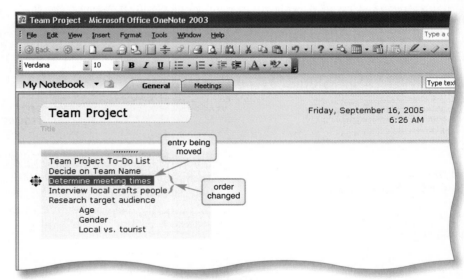

FIGURE 1-36

Using the above steps, you can change the order of the items in any list. You also can add new items to a list by clicking the position for the new item, typing the item, and then pressing the ENTER key. To delete an item, point in front of the item so that the paragraph handle appears, click the paragraph handle to select the item, and then press the DELETE key.

Creating an Outline

When typing a list, as soon as you type a number and press the TAB key, OneNote assumes you are creating an outline. From that point on, OneNote automatically will make the appropriate entries in the outline. You simply press the ENTER key at the end of each line. The next line initially will be at the same level as the previous line. To move to a higher level, press the BACKSPACE key. To move to a lower level, press the TAB key. The following steps show how to create an outline.

To Create an Outline

1

• **Click the Course Notes tab to move to the Course Notes page.**

• **Click the approximate position of the first C in Consumer Characteristics in Figure 1-37, type** Consumer Characteristics **on the first line in the container, press the ENTER key, type** 1. **on the second line, and then press the TAB key.**

OneNote creates an outline. The number 1 is moved to the left.

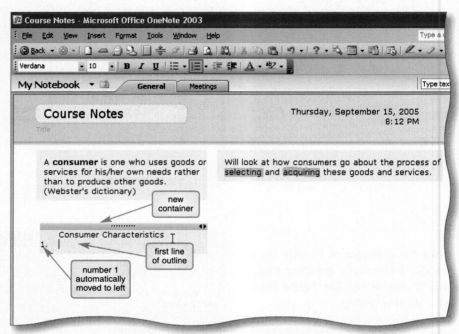

FIGURE 1-37

2

• **Type** Culture and values **as the first line of the outline.**

The first line of the outline is entered (Figure 1-38).

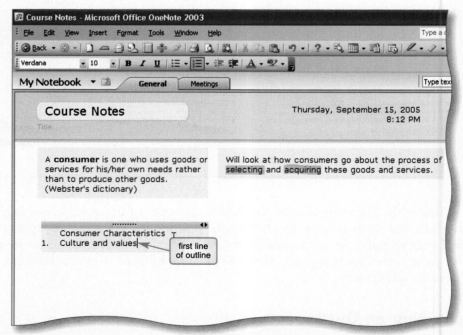

FIGURE 1-38

3

• **Press the ENTER key.**

OneNote inserts the number 2 for the second line of the outline (Figure 1-39).

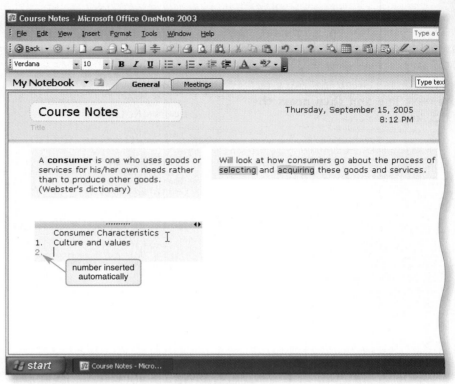

FIGURE 1-39

4

• **Press the TAB key.**

• **OneNote removes the number 2 and replaces it with the letter a (Figure 1-40). The next entry is indented appropriately.**

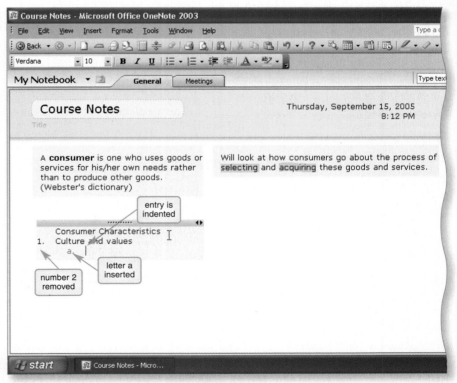

FIGURE 1-40

5

• **Type** Essential characteristics **as the next line and then press the ENTER key.**

• **Type** Underlying beliefs **as the next line and then press the ENTER key.**

The next two lines are entered (Figure 1-41). The letter c appears on the next line.

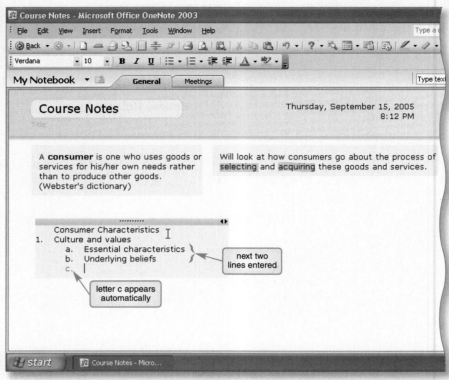

FIGURE 1-41

6

• **Press the BACKSPACE key twice.**

The letter c no longer appears (Figure 1-42). The number 2 appears in the appropriate location. The insertion point also is in the appropriate location.

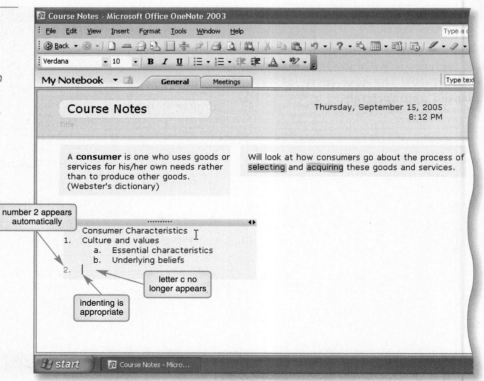

FIGURE 1-42

7

• **Using the techniques in Steps 2 through 6, enter the rest of the outline as shown in Figure 1-43.**

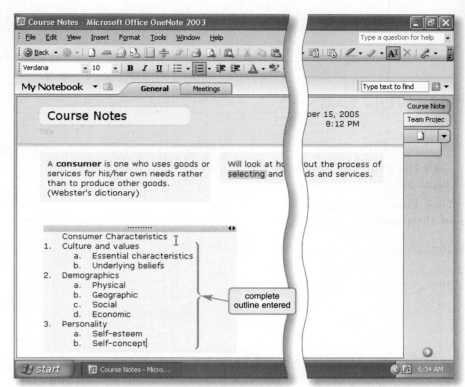

FIGURE 1-43

If the contents of a page do not fit on the screen, a **scroll bar** appears. The box in the scroll bar is called a **scroll box**, and the arrows at either end of the scroll bar are called **scroll arrows**. To move up or down within the document, you can drag the scroll box in the appropriate direction. You also can click the appropriate scroll arrow.

Using Note Flags

You can mark paragraphs in your notes for later action by placing special symbols, called **note flags**, in front of the notes. Several types of note flags are available: To Do, Important, Question, Remember for Later, and Definition. The check box represents a **To Do note flag**. A check mark in a To Do note flag indicates that the task already has been completed. The question mark represents a **Question note flag**, which represents an item to investigate further. The star represents the **Important note flag**, which is any note to mark for the future as being especially important. Not only do the note flags call attention to the corresponding notes, but you also can create a **Note Flags summary**, which is a list of only those notes to which you have attached a note flag. In addition to the built-in collection of note flags, you also can create custom note flags.

Adding Note Flags

The easiest way to add a note flag is to use the Note Flags toolbar. Thus, if you are adding note flags, the first step is to make sure the Note Flags toolbar is

More About

Custom Note Flags

To help you use your notes more efficiently, you can create your own custom note flags. To create a custom note flag, click Format on the menu bar, point to Note Flags on the Format menu, and then click Customize My Note Flags on the Note Flags submenu. Click the note flag you wish to customize and then click the Modify button in the Customize My Note Flags task pane. OneNote displays the Modify Note Flag dialog box. To change the name, type the new name in the Display name text box. To customize the format of the note flag, make the appropriate changes to Symbol, Font Color, and/or Highlight Color. When you have finished, click the OK button.

displayed. You then can add a note flag to a paragraph by clicking anywhere within the paragraph and then clicking the appropriate note flag. After you have added all the desired note flags, you can remove the Note Flags toolbar from the window to save room. The following steps show how to add the note flags.

To Add Note Flags

1

• **Click the page tab for the Team Project page.**

• **Click View on the menu bar and then point to Toolbars.**

The View menu and the Toolbars submenu appear (Figure 1-44). Your menu choices may be slightly different.

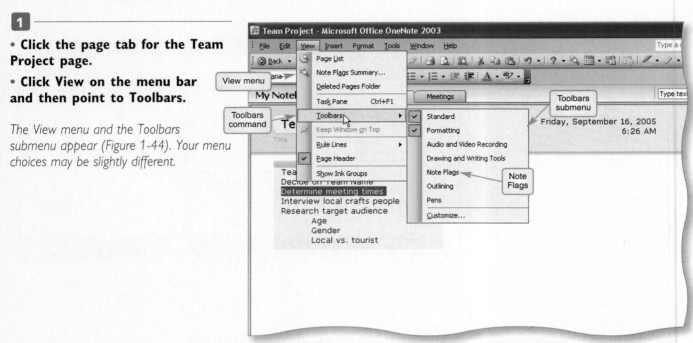

FIGURE 1-44

2

• **If Note Flags does not have a check mark to its left, click Note Flags on the Toolbars submenu.**

• **Click anywhere in the Decide on Team Name entry.**

The Note Flags toolbar appears (Figure 1-45). (Yours may be in a different location.) The insertion point is within the Decide on Team Name entry.

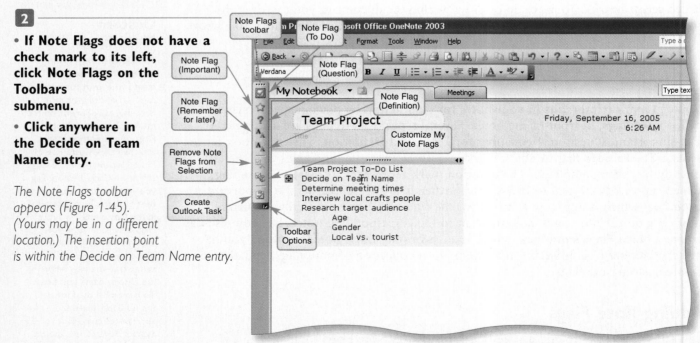

FIGURE 1-45

3

• **Click the Note Flag (To Do) button on the Note Flags toolbar.**

A To Do note flag appears to the left of the Decide on Team Name entry (Figure 1-46).

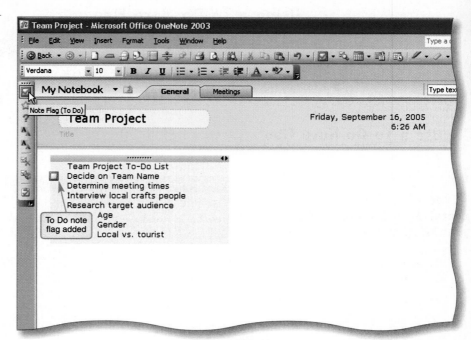

FIGURE 1-46

4

• **Click anywhere in the Determine meeting times entry and then click the Note Flag (To Do) button on the Note Flags toolbar.**

• **Click anywhere in the Interview local crafts people entry and then click the Note Flag (Question) button on the Note Flags toolbar.**

• **Click anywhere in the Research target audience entry and then click the Note Flag (Important) button on the Note Flags toolbar.**

• **Click View on the menu bar, point to Toolbars, and then click Note Flags on the Toolbars submenu to remove the Note Flags toolbar.**

The note flags are added (Figure 1-47). The Note Flags toolbar no longer appears.

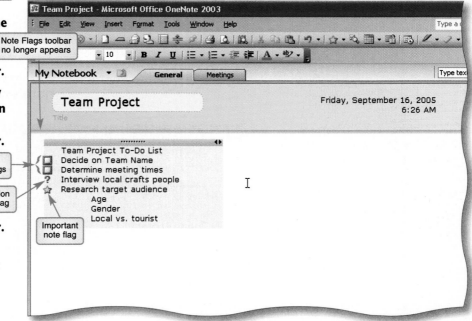

FIGURE 1-47

Other Ways
1. On Format menu point to Note Flags, click desired flag on Note Flags submenu.

If you do not mind giving up the space occupied by the Note Flags toolbar, you could leave it on the screen. It then would be readily available whenever you want to add other note flags.

Using a To Do Note Flag

A To Do note flag is in the shape of a check box. To indicate that the corresponding task is complete, place a check mark in the box. The following steps first add a team name to the page and then place a check mark in the To Do note flag that precedes the Decide on Team Name task.

To Use a To Do Note Flag

1

• **Type** Team Name: FAB Three **in a container in the approximate position shown in Figure 1-48.**

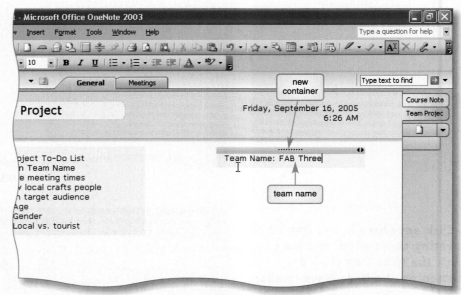

FIGURE 1-48

2

Click the To Do note flag to the left of Decide on Team Name.

The note flag now contains a check mark, which indicates the task is complete (Figure 1-49).

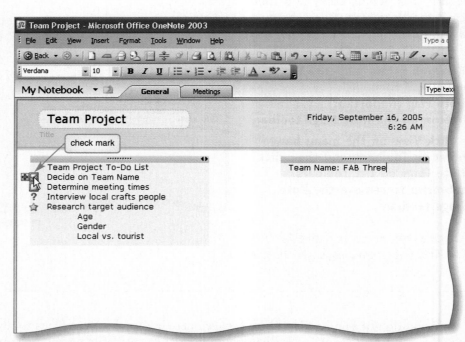

FIGURE 1-49

Adding Pictures

You can add pictures and other images to your notes. Once you have added them, you can move them and resize them just as you move and resize any other container. The following steps add pictures to your notes. The steps assume that the pictures are stored in a folder called Pictures on drive C (the computer's hard disk).

To Add Pictures

1

• **Click near the left side of the screen slightly below the container for the list.**

• **Click Insert on the menu bar and then point to Picture on the Insert menu.**

The Insert menu and Picture submenu appear (Figure 1-50).

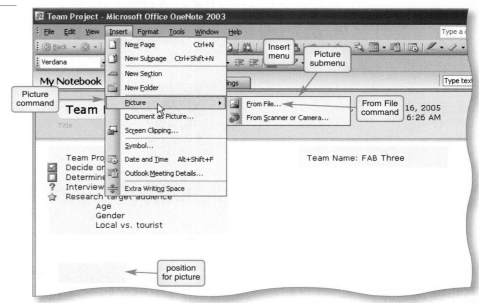

FIGURE 1-50

2

• **Click From File on the Picture submenu.**

• **When the Insert Picture dialog box is displayed, navigate to the folder containing the pictures.**

The pictures appear in the Insert Picture dialog box (Figure 1-51).

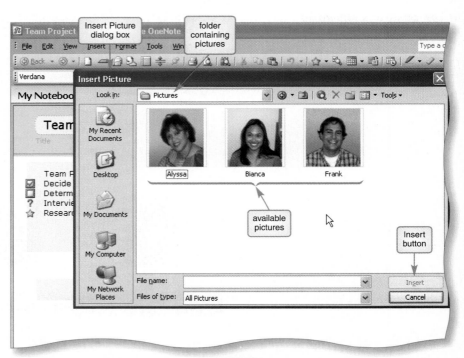

FIGURE 1-51

3

• **Click the picture named Alyssa and then click the Insert button.**

The picture for Alyssa is added to the page (Figure 1-52).

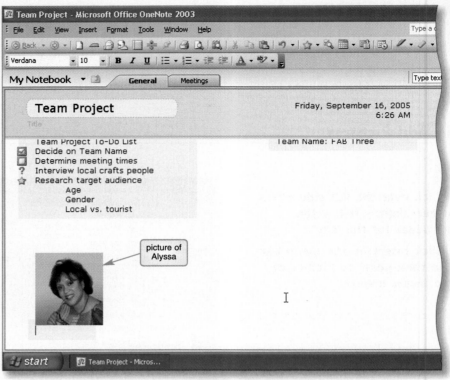

FIGURE 1-52

4

• **Use the technique shown in Steps 1 through 3 to add the pictures for Bianca and Frank in the positions shown in Figure 1-53.**

The pictures are added.

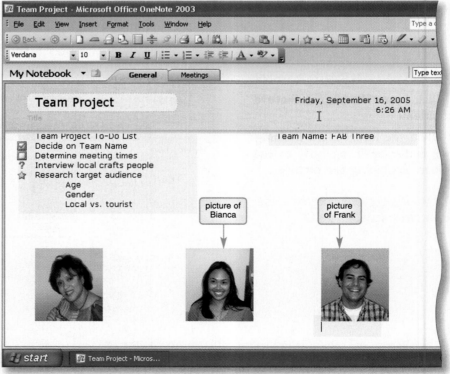

FIGURE 1-53

5

• **Type** Alyssa, Bianca, **and** Frank **below their respective pictures (Figure 1-54).**

The names are added.

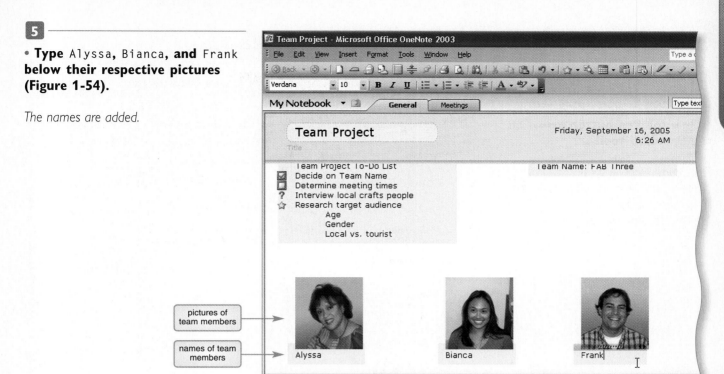

FIGURE 1-54

Drawing and Handwriting

In OneNote, you can draw sketches and use handwriting to write notes by using what is termed **electronic ink**. In the process, you can choose which **pen** you want to use to draw or write. You can specify both the color and pen thickness. You also can use an electronic **eraser** to erase your drawing or writing.

You can use a mouse or other pointing device for the drawings and handwriting on any computer. The most convenient environment for drawing and writing, however is the Tablet PC. With the Tablet PC, you can draw or write directly on the screen with the special included pen.

Adding a Drawing

The Pen button on the Standard toolbar is used to add a drawing. When the Pen is in use, the mouse pointer becomes a small dot. Dragging the dot pointer creates the drawing. Because the drawing will use the currently selected pen color and thickness, it is a good idea to make sure you have selected the color and thickness you want just before you click the Pen button. To do so, click the Pen button arrow and then click the desired color and thickness. The steps on the next page illustrate the process of creating a drawing.

More About

Pen Mode

On a Tablet PC, the Pen mode determines whether the Tablet PC treats the "ink" you place on the screen with the stylus as handwriting or a drawing. You can change the Pen mode by clicking Tools on the menu bar, clicking Pen Mode on the Tools menu, and then clicking the desired mode. The possible modes are Create Both Handwriting and Drawings, Create Handwriting Only, and Create Drawings Only. If you select Create Both Handwriting and Drawings, the Tablet PC will try to determine whether the content that you place on the screen is handwriting or simply a drawing.

To Add a Drawing

1

• **Click the Course Notes tab.**

• **Click the Pen button arrow on the Standard toolbar.**

The Course Notes page is displayed (Figure 1-55). The list of available pens and highlighters appears.

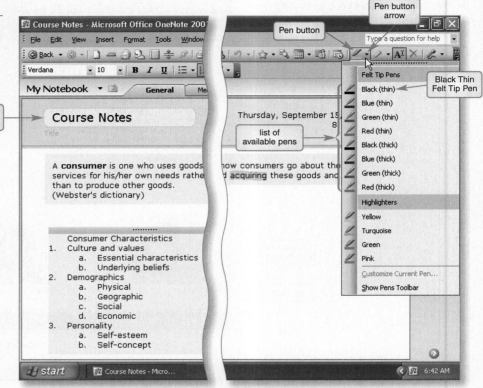

FIGURE 1-55

2

• **Click Black (thin) in the Felt Tip Pens area.**

Black (thin) is selected (Figure 1-56).

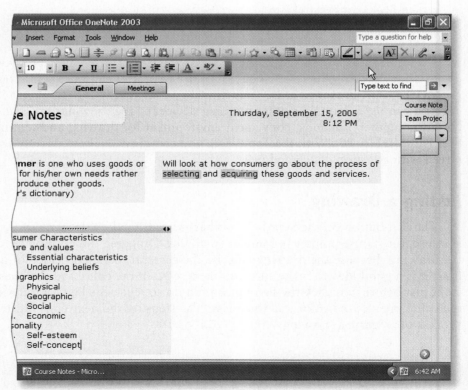

FIGURE 1-56

3

• **Using a mouse or other pointing device, sketch the graph shown in Figure 1-57 in the approximate position shown in the figure.**

The graph is added to the page.

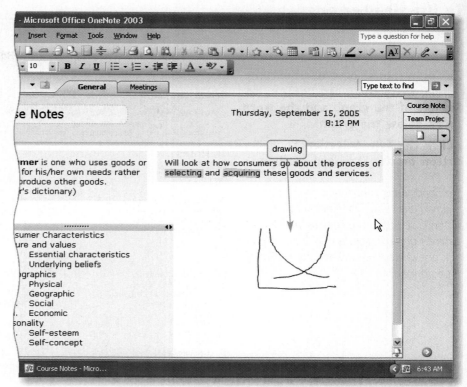

FIGURE 1-57

You now can use the pen pointer to continue drawing or to write notes. Upon completion of a drawing, click the Type/Selection Tool button to return the pen pointer to the normal mouse pointer.

Using Handwriting

You also can handwrite notes using the Pen button as illustrated in the steps on the next page. These steps assume that you already have clicked the Pen button on the Standard toolbar.

Other Ways

1. On Tools menu point to Drawing and Writing Tools, click appropriate command on Drawing and Writing Tools submenu

More About

Inserting More Writing Space

When you are typing text, OneNote automatically will add any additional space necessary to accommodate the text. This is not necessarily the case when you are drawing or using handwriting. If OneNote does not add the space you need automatically, you can add space by clicking the Insert Extra Writing Space button on the Standard toolbar or by clicking Insert on the menu bar and then clicking Extra Writing Space on the Insert menu.

To Use Handwriting

1

• **Using a mouse or other pointing device, write the word** Dollars **to the left of the graph and the word** Units **below the graph.**

• **Click the Type/Selection Tool button on the Standard toolbar.**

The handwriting is added to the drawing (Figure 1-58). The Type/Selection Tool button is selected. The lines on the drawing currently are exaggerated. As soon as you click elsewhere, they will assume a normal appearance.

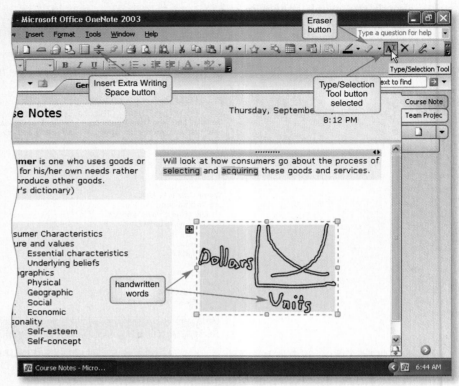

FIGURE 1-58

2

• **Click somewhere outside the container containing the drawing.**

The drawing and the handwritten words assume a normal appearance (Figure 1-59).

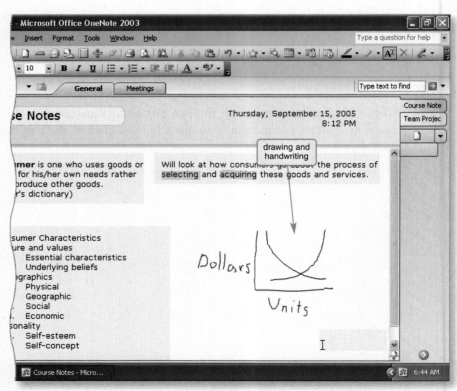

FIGURE 1-59

Other Ways

1. On Tools menu click Drawing and Writing Tools

If you are using a Tablet PC, two differences in entering handwriting exist. First, because you use a pen to write directly on the screen, you are apt to be able to do a better job drawing and writing. Second, OneNote takes advantage of the handwriting recognition technology that is part of the version of Windows XP for the Tablet PC to give you the capability to convert your handwriting to text. All you have to do is right-click the container that contains your handwriting and then choose Convert Handwriting to Text on the shortcut menu.

If you make a mistake when drawing or writing, you can correct it by clicking the Eraser button on the Standard toolbar (see Figure 1-58). You then can drag the mouse pointer, whose shape has become an eraser, over the desired handwriting or drawings to erase.

If you ever find that you do not have sufficient writing space at the bottom of your page to add your drawing or handwriting, you can add more space by using the Insert Extra Writing Space button on the Standard toolbar.

Adding a Subpage

Rather than continually adding to the bottom of a page, you might find it more convenient to add a subpage. Because a subpage has a tab, you easily can move to the subpage to view its contents. You add a subpage for an existing page by using the New Subpage tab. The following steps show how to add a subpage to the Team Project page.

To Add a Subpage

1

• **Click the Team Project tab.**

The Team Project page appears (Figure 1-60).

FIGURE 1-60

More About

Pen Pressure Sensitivity

On a Tablet PC, it is possible to enable pen pressure sensitivity. With pen pressure sensitivity enabled, the harder you press when writing or drawing with the stylus, the darker your writing or drawing will appear. To enable pen pressure sensitivity, click Tools on the menu bar, click Options on the Tools menu, click Handwriting, and then be sure the Use pen pressure sensitivity check box is selected. To disable pen pressure sensitivity, use the same steps, but be sure the Use pen pressure sensitivity check box is not selected.

2

• **Point to the New Subpage tab.**

A ScreenTip appears (Figure 1-61).

3

• **Click the New Subpage tab to create a new subpage.**

A new subpage appears.

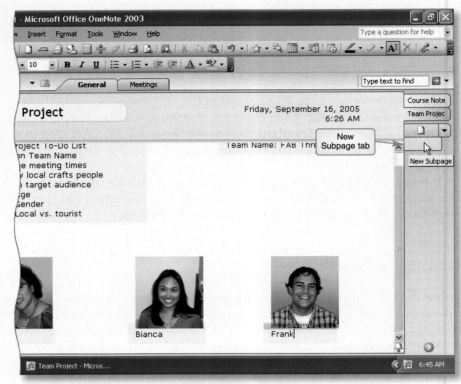

FIGURE 1-61

The new subpage now is available for use. You can use it just like you would use a page. The only difference is that the subpage shares the page title with the original page, rather than having its own title.

Adding a Table

Although you cannot add true tables to your notes, you can add a structure in which the contents are aligned in rows and columns, similar to a table. The structure is a called a **horizontal outline**. You can add a horizontal outline by using the TAB key, the ENTER key, and the BACKSPACE key, as illustrated in the following steps.

To Add a Table

1

• **Click near the upper-left corner of the new subpage.**

• **Type** Task **as the first entry in the container, press the TAB key, and then type** Person Responsible **as the second entry.**

The new subpage is displayed (Figure 1-62). A new container appears. It contains the first row of a two-column table.

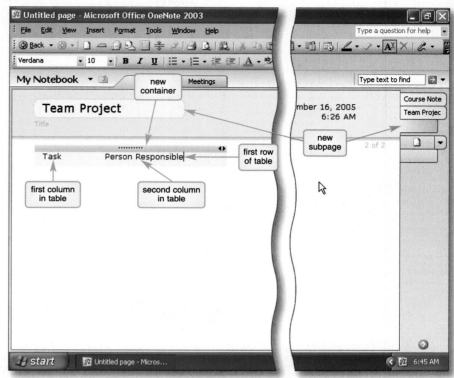

FIGURE 1-62

2

• **Press the ENTER key.**

The insertion point moves to the second row in the second column (Figure 1-63).

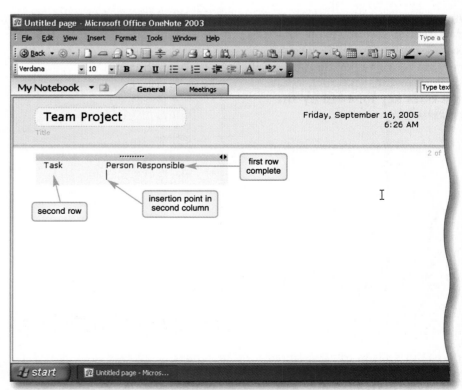

FIGURE 1-63

3

• **Press the BACKSPACE key.**

The insertion point moves back to the first column (Figure 1-64).

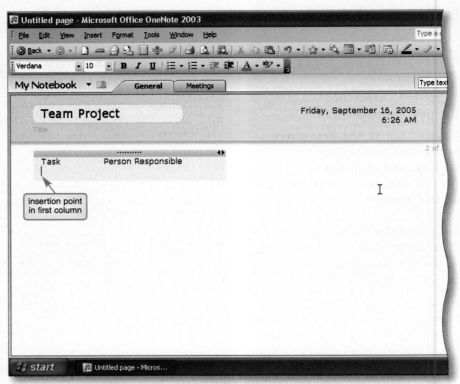

FIGURE 1-64

4

• **Enter the remaining rows in the table as shown in Figure 1-65. To move from the first column in a row to the second, press the TAB key. To move from the second column in a row to the first column in the next row, press the ENTER key followed by the BACKSPACE key.**

The contents of the table are entered.

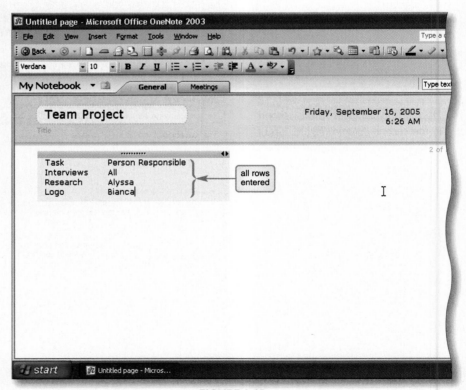

FIGURE 1-65

Printing Notes

You can print your notes at anytime. You also can change print settings to affect the way the notes print.

Printing All Pages in a Section

Clicking the Print button on the Standard toolbar prints only the current page. Often, you will want to print all the pages in a section. To do so, you need to use the Print command on the File menu. The following steps use the Print command to print all the pages in the section.

To Print All Pages in a Section

1

• **Click the Course Notes tab.**

• **Click File on the menu bar.**

The File menu appears (Figure 1-66).

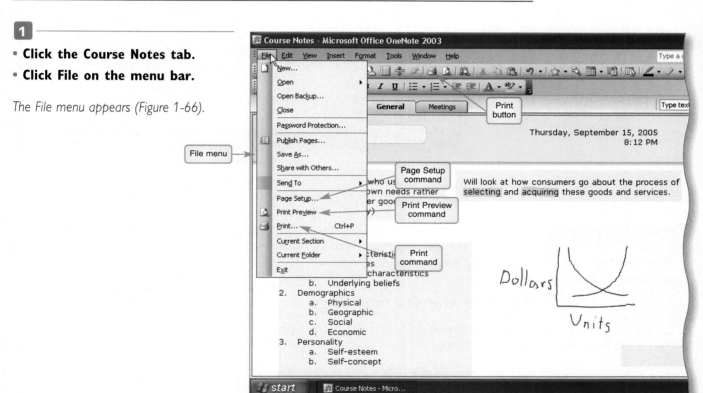

FIGURE 1-66

2

• **Click Print on the File menu.**

• **When the Print dialog box is displayed, click All in the Page Range area.**

The Print dialog box appears (Figure 1-67). Because the All option button is selected, all pages in the section will be printed.

3

• **Click the Print button in the Print dialog box.**

The pages print. They look like the printed pages shown in Figures 1-1 and 1-2 on pages ONE 5 through ONE 7.

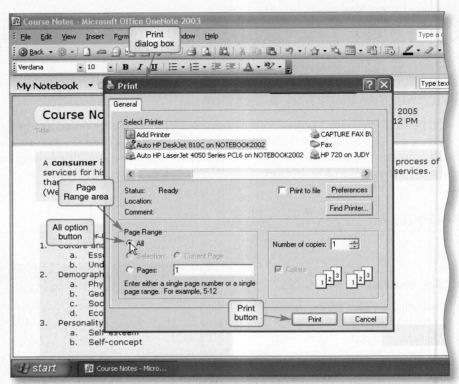

FIGURE 1-67

A command for printing all the pages in all the sections in your notebook is not available. You need to repeat the above steps for each section if you want to print the pages in more than one section.

Printing the Current Page

You also can print just the current page. The following step shows how to print the current page.

TO PRINT THE CURRENT PAGE

1. Click the Print button on the Standard toolbar (shown in Figure 1-66 on the previous page).

Showing Rule Lines

Paper in a physical notebook can be blank or lined. You can include these lines, called **rule lines**, on the pages in your notebook by selecting the Show Rule Lines check box in the Page Setup task pane (Figure 1-68). The following steps illustrate how to show the rule lines.

TO SHOW RULE LINES

1. Click File on the menu bar and then click Page Setup on the File menu.
2. Click the Line style box arrow in the Page Setup task pane and then select the desired style (for example, College Ruled).
3. Close the Page Setup task pane by clicking its Close button.

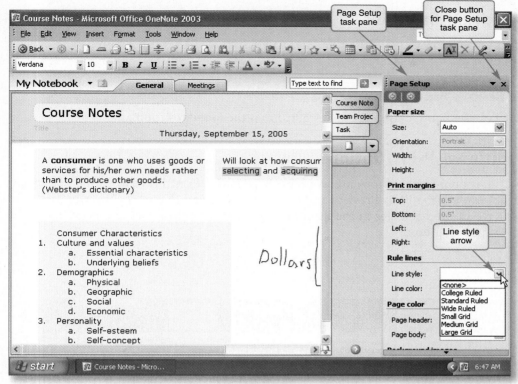

FIGURE 1-68

Rule lines now will appear on the page (Figure 1-69). If you are not using any of the other options in the Page Setup task pane, there is a shortcut to producing rule lines. You simply can click the Show/Hide Rule Lines button on the Standard toolbar. On a Tablet PC, you normally will include rule lines. In other environments, you typically do not include them, although this is a matter of personal preference. If you would prefer a different style of rule lines, click View on the menu bar, point to Rule Lines, and then click the style you want on the Rule Lines submenu.

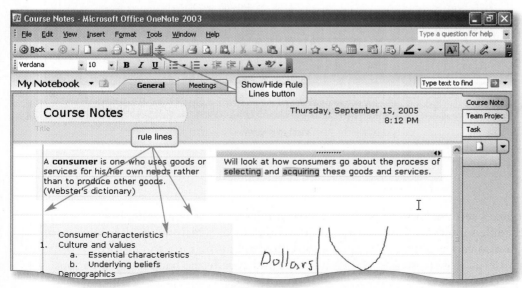

FIGURE 1-69

Removing Rule Lines

If you no longer want the rule lines to be displayed, you can remove them as shown in the following step.

TO REMOVE RULE LINES

1. Click the Show/Hide Rule Lines button on the Standard toolbar.

Additional Print Options

Additional print options are available if you click Print Preview on the File menu, which displays the Print Preview and Settings dialog box (Figure 1-70). You can make the desired changes in the Print Settings area, and then click the Print button in the Print dialog box.

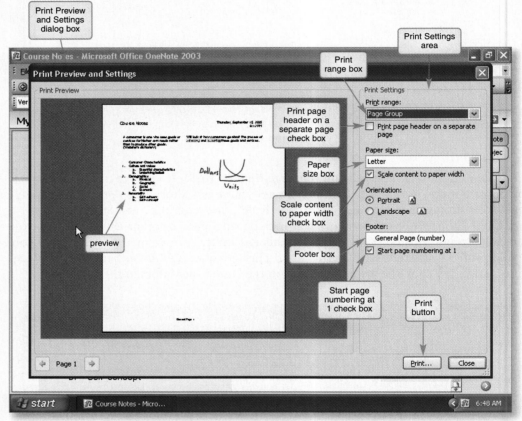

FIGURE 1-70

Performing Backups

You can set OneNote to perform automatic backups of your notebook at regularly scheduled intervals. You can specify the intervals at which the backups are to occur. You also can specify the location where the backup files are to be stored. For information on how to schedule such backups and specify the backup file locations, see the Appendix.

You also can force OneNote to perform an immediate backup as illustrated in the following steps.

TO PERFORM AN IMMEDIATE BACKUP

1. Click Tools on the menu bar and then click Options on the Tools menu to display the Options dialog box.
2. In the Options dialog box, click Backup in the Category list and then click the Backup Now button.
3. Click the OK button.

A backup copy of your notebook now will exist. It will have the current time and date associated with it. If you later want to open this backup file, you can do so, as shown in the following steps.

TO OPEN A BACKUP FILE

1. Click File on the menu bar and then click Open Backup on the File menu.
2. Select the backup folder you want to open and then click the Open button in the File Open dialog box. (If more than one folder is listed, use the date to determine the one you want.)
3. Select the section you want to open and then click the Open button in the File Open dialog box.

OneNote Help System

At anytime while you are using OneNote, you can get answers to questions using the OneNote Help system. You can activate the OneNote Help system by using the Type a question for help box on the menu bar or by clicking Help on the menu bar (Figure 1-71 on the next page). Used properly, this form of online assistance can increase your productivity and reduce your frustrations by minimizing the time you spend learning how to use OneNote.

The following section shows how to get answers to your questions using the Type a question for help box. Additional information on using the OneNote Help system is available in Table 1-2 on page ONE 54.

Obtaining Help Using the Type a Question for Help Box on the Menu Bar

The Type a question for help box on the right side of the menu bar lets you type free-form questions such as *How do I delete a note* or key terms such as *page* or *note flag*. OneNote responds by displaying a list of topics related to the question or terms you entered. The steps on the next page show how to use the Type a question for help box to obtain information on deleting a note.

More About

The Quick Reference

For a table that lists how to complete the tasks covered in this book using the mouse, menu, shortcut menu, and keyboard, see the Quick Reference Summary at the back of this book or visit the OneNote 2003 Quick Reference Web page (scsite.com/one2003/qr).

To Obtain Help Using the Type a Question for Help Box

1

• **Type** how do I delete a note **in the Type a question for help box on the right side of the menu bar (Figure 1-71).**

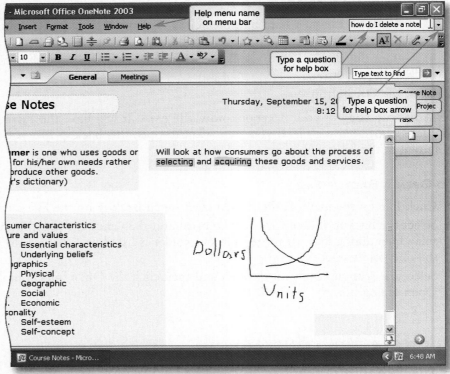

FIGURE 1-71

2

• **Press the ENTER key.**

OneNote displays the Search Results task pane with a list of topics related to the question, how do I delete a note (Figure 1-72). Your list may be different.

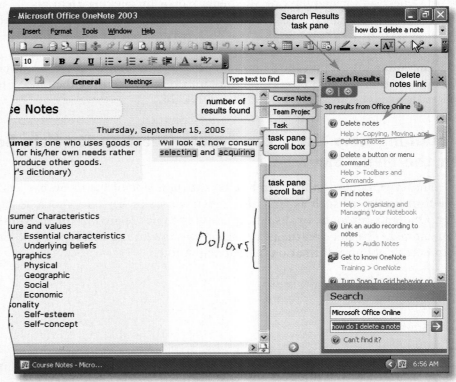

FIGURE 1-72

3

• **Click the Delete notes link in the Search Results task pane.**

OneNote opens the Microsoft Office OneNote Help window that provides information about deleting notes (Figure 1-73). You can click the link for a topic in the window to see additional information on that topic. Clicking the Show All link allows you to see additional information on all topics in the window.

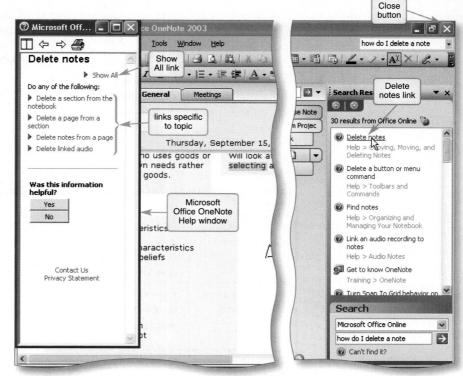

FIGURE 1-73

4

• **Click the Show All link on the right side of the Microsoft Office OneNote Help window to expand all the links in the window.**

• **Double-click the Microsoft Office OneNote Help title bar to maximize the window.**

The links in the Microsoft Office OneNote Help window are expanded. OneNote maximized the window that provides Help information about deleting notes (Figure 1-74).

5

• **Click the Close button on the title bar to close the Help window.**

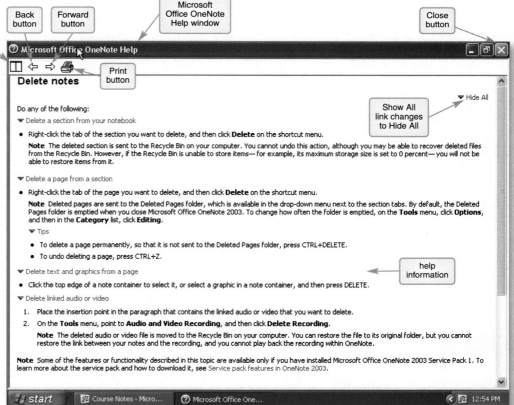

FIGURE 1-74

The Microsoft OneNote Help window closes.

Use the buttons in the upper-left corner of the Microsoft Office OneNote Help window (Figure 1-74 on the previous page) to navigate through the Help system, change the display, and print the contents of the window.

As you enter questions and terms in the Type a question for help box, OneNote adds them to its list. Thus, if you click the Type a question for help box arrow (shown in Figure 1-71 on page ONE 52), OneNote will display a list of previously entered questions and terms.

Table 1-2 summarizes the types of help available through commands on the Help menu.

Table 1-2   OneNote Help System

TYPE	DESCRIPTION	HOW TO ACTIVATE
Microsoft Office OneNote Help	Displays OneNote Help task pane. Answers questions or searches for terms that you type in your own words.	Click Microsoft Office OneNote Help on the Help menu.
Type a question for help box	Answers questions or searches for terms that you type in your own words.	Type a question or term in the Type a question for help box on the menu bar and then press the ENTER key.
Table of Contents	Groups Help topics by general categories in table of contents form. Use when you know only the general category of the topic in question.	Click Microsoft Office OneNote Help on the Help menu and then click the Table of Contents link in the OneNote Help task pane.
Keyboard Shortcuts	Used to find a list of keyboard shortcuts for many OneNote operations.	Click Keyboard Shortcuts on the Help menu.
Microsoft Office Online	Used to access technical resources on the Web.	Click Microsoft Office Online on the Help menu.
Check for Updates	Used to check for and download free product enhancements on the Web.	Click Check for Updates on the Help menu.
Detect and Repair	Automatically finds and fixes errors in the application.	Click Detect and Repair on the Help menu.

Quitting OneNote

After you have made all the changes to the notebook, Project 1 is complete and you are ready to quit OneNote. The following step shows how to quit OneNote.

To Quit OneNote

1 **Click the Close button on the right side of the title bar (shown in Figure 1-73 on the previous page).**

Project Summary

In creating the pages and subpage in this project, you gained a broad knowledge of OneNote. First, you were introduced to starting OneNote. You learned about the OneNote window and how to work with sections. You learned how to enter a note in a container on a blank page. You then learned how to move and resize the container. You learned how to format and how to highlight characters in a note.

The project presented information about new pages in a notebook and illustrated creating a new page. You learned how to create lists and outlines. Next, you saw how to add note flags as well as how to use a To Do note flag. You learned to add pictures to your notes, as well as how to use the pen to draw sketches and to handwrite notes. You learned how to add a subpage and also how to create a table-like structure using a horizontal outline. You saw various options for printing your notes and also learned how to perform a backup. Finally, you learned how to use the OneNote Help system to answer your questions.

What You Should Know

Having completed this project, you now should be able to perform the tasks below. The tasks are listed in the same order they were presented in this project. For a list of the buttons, menus, toolbars, and commands introduced in this project, see the Quick Reference Summary at the back of this book, and refer to the Page Number column.

1. Start OneNote (ONE 8)
2. Customize the OneNote Window (ONE 9)
3. Close a Section (ONE 15)
4. Delete a Section (ONE 16)
5. Rename a Section (ONE 16)
6. Create a Section (ONE 16)
7. Open a Section (ONE 17)
8. Change a Section Color (ONE 18)
9. Add a Page Title (ONE 18)
10. Add a Note and Container to a Blank Page (ONE 19)
11. Move a Container (ONE 20)
12. Resize a Container (ONE 21)
13. Delete a Container (ONE 23)
14. Split a Container (ONE 23)
15. Add an Additional Note (ONE 23)
16. Format Characters (ONE 24)
17. Highlight Characters (ONE 25)
18. Add a New Page (ONE 26)
19. Add a List (ONE 27)
20. Move Items in a List (ONE 29)
21. Create an Outline (ONE 30)
22. Add Note Flags (ONE 34)
23. Use a To Do Note Flag (ONE 36)
24. Add Pictures (ONE 37)
25. Add a Drawing (ONE 40)
26. Use Handwriting (ONE 42)
27. Add a Subpage (ONE 43)
28. Add a Table (ONE 45)
29. Print All Pages in a Section (ONE 47)
30. Print the Current Page (ONE 48)
31. Show Rule Lines (ONE 48)
32. Remove Rule Lines (ONE 50)
33. Perform an Immediate Backup (ONE 51)
34. Open a Backup File (ONE 51)
35. Obtain Help Using the Type a Question for Help Box (ONE 52)
36. Quit OneNote (ONE 54)

Learn It Online

Instructions: To complete the Learn It Online exercises, start your browser, click the Address bar, and then enter the Web address scsite.com/one2003/learn. When the OneNote 2003 Learn It Online page is displayed, follow the instructions in the exercises below. Each exercise has instructions for printing your results, either for your own records or for submission to your instructor.

1 Project Reinforcement TF, MC, and SA

Below OneNote Project 1, click the Project Reinforcement link. Print the quiz by clicking Print on the File menu. Answer each question.

2 Flash Cards

Below OneNote Project 1, click the Flash Cards link and read the instructions. Type 20 (or a number specified by your instructor) in the Number of playing cards text box, type your name in the Enter your Name text box, and then click the Flip Card button. When the flash card is displayed, read the question and then click the ANSWER box arrow to select an answer. Flip through Flash Cards. If your score is 15 (75%) correct or greater, click Print on the File menu to print your results. If your score is less than 15 (75%) correct, then redo this exercise by clicking the Replay button.

3 Practice Test

Below OneNote Project 1, click the Practice Test link. Answer each question, enter your first and last name at the bottom of the page, and then click the Grade Test button. When the graded practice test is displayed on your screen, click Print on the File menu to print a hard copy. Continue to take practice tests until you score 80% or better.

4 Who Wants To Be a Computer Genius?

Below OneNote Project 1, click the Computer Genius link. Read the instructions, enter your first and last name at the bottom of the page, and then click the PLAY button. When your score is displayed, click the PRINT RESULTS link to print a hard copy.

5 Wheel of Terms

Below OneNote Project 1, click the Wheel of Terms link. Read the instructions, and then enter your first and last name and your school name. Click the PLAY button. When your score is displayed, right-click the score and then click Print on the shortcut menu to print a hard copy.

6 Crossword Puzzle Challenge

Below OneNote Project 1, click the Crossword Puzzle Challenge link. Read the instructions, and then enter your first and last name. Click the SUBMIT button. Work the crossword puzzle. When you are finished, click the Submit button. When the crossword puzzle is redisplayed, click the Print button to print a hard copy.

7 Tips and Tricks

Below OneNote Project 1, click the Tips and Tricks link. Click a topic that pertains to Project 1. Right-click the information and then click Print on the shortcut menu. Construct a brief example of what the information relates to in OneNote to confirm you understand how to use the tip or trick.

8 Newsgroups

Below OneNote Project 1, click the Newsgroups link. Click a topic that pertains to Project 1. Print three comments.

9 Expanding Your Horizons

Below OneNote Project 1, click the Expanding Your Horizons link. Click a topic that pertains to Project 1. Print the information. Construct a brief example of what the information relates to in OneNote to confirm you understand the contents of the article.

10 Search Sleuth

Below OneNote Project 1, click the Search Sleuth link. To search for a term that pertains to this project, select a term below the Project 1 title and then use the Google search engine at google.com (or any major search engine) to display and print two Web pages that present information on the term.

11 OneNote Online Training

Below OneNote Project 1, click the OneNote Online Training link. When your browser displays the Office on Microsoft.com Web page, click the OneNote link. Click one of the OneNote courses that covers one or more of the objectives listed at the beginning of the project on page ONE 4. Print the first page of the course before stepping through it.

12 Office Marketplace

Below OneNote Project 1, click the Office Marketplace link. When your browser displays the Office on Microsoft.com Web page, click the Office Marketplace link. Click a topic that relates to OneNote. Print the first page.

Apply Your Knowledge

1 Taking Notes in a Computer Science Course

Instructions: Jenny Sitts, also a student at Penn County Community College, is taking a course in database management this semester and is using OneNote to help her with the class. Start OneNote. Perform the following tasks:

1. Create a new section in your notebook. Name the section, Apply Your Knowledge.
2. Name the page, Class Notes.
3. Close the General and Meetings sections of the notebook.
4. Add the notes shown in Figure 1-75 to the Class Notes page.

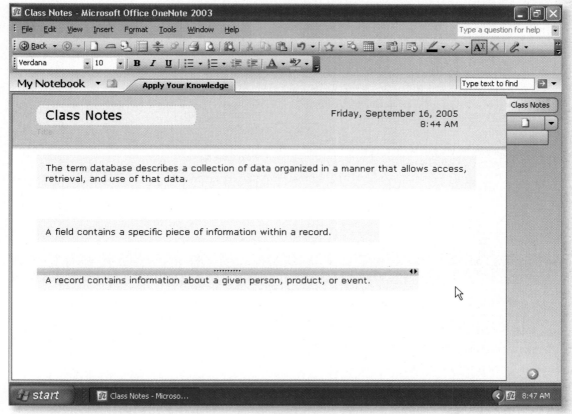

FIGURE 1-75

5. Bold the term, database, in the first note; the term, field, in the second note; and the the term, record, in the third note.
6. Print the Class Notes page.
7. Move the notes so that the third note appears before the second note.

(continued)

Apply Your Knowledge

Taking Notes in a Computer Science Course *(continued)*

8. Resize the notes to the approximate sizes and postions shown in Figure 1-76.
9. Add the container and the text shown in Figure 1-76.

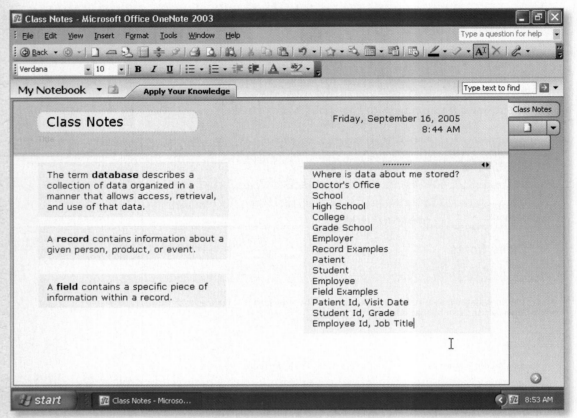

FIGURE 1-76

10. Print the Class Notes page.
11. Indent the the three entries (High School, College, Grade School) below School.
12. Move the Grade School entry above the High School entry.
13. Highlight the question, Where is data about me stored?.
14. Print the Class Notes page.
15. Split the container into two containers. The split occurs beginning with the line, Record Examples.
16. Print the page.
17. Perform an immediate back up of OneNote.
18. Close the Apply Your Knowledge section.

In the Lab

1 Creating a To Do List

Problem: Cordelia Lee's advisor has encouraged her to apply for a scholarship offered by a local organization. Because she realizes that it is critical that the application be completed correctly and on time, she decides to use OneNote to keep a list of the scholarship requirements. The scholarship requires the following: transcript from the registrar's office, a letter of reference from her advisor, a letter of reference from one other professor, a completed application form, a personal essay, and a projected course schedule for the next year.

Instructions: Start OneNote. Perform the following tasks:

1. Create a new section in your notebook. Name the section, In The Lab 1. Close any other open sections.
2. Name the page, Scholarship Requirements.
3. Enter the list shown in Figure 1-77.

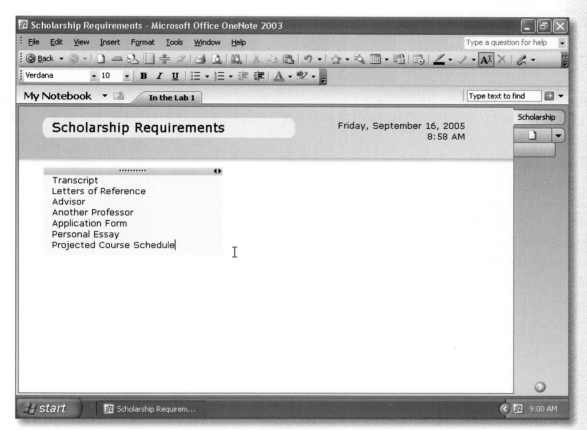

FIGURE 1-77

4. Print the current page.
5. Indent the two items below Letters of Reference.
6. Move the item, Application Form to the beginning of the list.

(continued)

In the Lab

Creating a To Do List *(continued)*

7. Print the current page.
8. Place the To Do note flag in front of every item on the list.
9. Indicate that the Transcript task has been completed.
10. Add a new container that contains the following:

   Deadline: February 28

11. Print the current page.
12. Move the container above the To Do List
13. Bold the word, Deadline, and the colon following it. Highlight the date (February 28) in yellow.
14. Place a picture of Cordelia to the right of the the To Do list. (Use one of the female pictures on the Data Disk.)
15. Print the current page.
16. Close the In The Lab 1 section.

2 Preparing a Lesson Plan

Problem: John Sanchez teaches Quantitative Problem Solving using PCs. Students learn to solve quantitative problems using Microsoft Excel and Microsoft Access. He uses OneNote to help him organize his ideas and prepare his lesson plans.

Instructions: Start OneNote. Perform the following tasks:

1. Create a new section named In The Lab 2. Close any other open sections.
2. Create a new page named Lesson Plan.
3. Create the page shown in Figure 1-78. The page has four containers and one drawing.
4. Print the page.
5. Close the In The Lab 2 section.

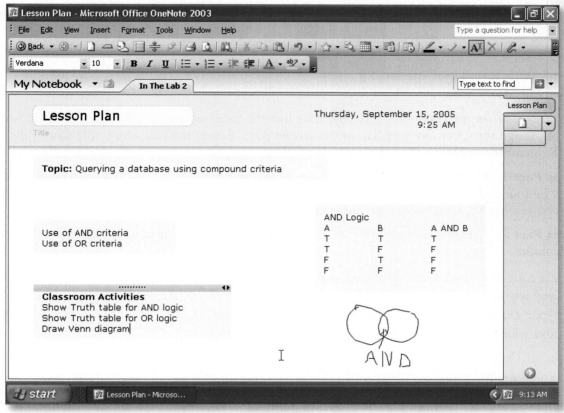

FIGURE 1-78

3 Beginning a Family History

Problem: Curt Jones maternal grandmother, Grace, is celebrating her 65th birthday next year. Curt has decided to surprise his grandmother with a book that contains her family history.

Instructions: Open OneNote and create a new section with the title In The Lab 3. The section should have one page titled Family History. Close any other open sections. When you have completed the instructions below, print the Family History section.

Instructions Part 1: Curt has done some basic research on the Web to help him get started with his family history. He has discovered that the four main sources of family information are:

1. Individual's own knowledge of family events
2. Interviews with family members

(continued)

Beginning a Family History *(continued)*

3. Household items (books, gifts, documents)
4. Previous research
   a. From family members
   b. From outside sources

   Create an outline on the Family History page that lists the four items above. Assign the To Do note flag to the first item. Assign the Question note flag to the second item. Assign the Important note flag to the third item. Assign the Remember for Later note flag to the fourth item.

Instructions Part 2: Create a subpage to store a list of household items and places where family history information may be found. A few of these items are: autograph books, bibles, photo albums, cookbooks, diaries, school papers, yearbooks, scrapbooks, and birth certificates.

Instructions Part 3: Create a subpage to store a list of basic questions that must be answered. Some of these questions include:

- Is there a copy of Grace's birth certificate and marriage certificate?
- When and where were Grace's parents born?
- Has anyone else in the family ever conducted any family research?
- When and where were Grace's brothers and sisters born?

   Close the In The Lab 3 section.

Cases and Places

The difficulty of these case studies varies:
■ are the least difficult and ■■ are the most difficult. The last exercise is a group exercise.

1 ■ As any comparison shopper knows, food prices vary dramatically from one store to another. Make a list of six specific items that you purchase frequently. Include the size or weight of each item and then obtain prices for each item from at least two sources. Be sure you obtain prices on identical products. You can visit stores to obtain prices or check the ads in your local paper. Create a section in OneNote named C&P 1 and use the horizontal outline feature to record the comparison.

2 ■ You and two friends have decided to participate in the city-wide garage sale/flea market and sell items you no longer want or need. The city charges a fee for the space you rent. You and your friends are responsible for any other costs, such as renting a truck to transport the items. Determine what needs to be done to get ready for the garage sale and then enter the items in OneNote. Be sure to include a subpage that identifies which individual is responsible for each task. Create a section named C&P 2 to store your notes.

3 ■■ You have decided to earn some extra money by caring for small pets in their own homes when their owners are away on short trips. Use OneNote to prepare a sample flyer advertising your new business. You will use the sample created in OneNote as a basis for discussion with a firm that specializes in designing and printing flyers and brochures. Be sure to include a picture of yourself. (You can either use one of the pictures on the Data Disk or use your own picture.) Create a section named C&P 3 to store your sample flyer.

4 ■■ You need to create a Web page that will include information about you for the career placement office at school. The office needs to have the following included on the Web page: your picture, your name, your major, your intended date of graduation, a brief description of work experience relevant to your major, and a list of school activities. You do not know how to create Web pages, but your friend does, so you decide to use OneNote to prepare a sample Web page. Your friend then can use the sample to create the Web page for you. (You can either use one of the pictures on the Data Disk or use your own picture.) Create a section named C&P 4 to store your sample Web page.

5 ■■ **Working Together** Microsoft Office OneNote is designed to work with Tablet PCs. Work with a group of your classmates to form a team. Have each team member research the features, price, and accessories of one brand of Tablet PC by looking through newspapers, magazines, searching the Web, and/or visiting an electronics or computer store. Instruct each team member to use OneNote to summarize his or her findings. Then, meet as a group to compare your findings and prepare an oral presentation to summarize the comparisons.

Organizing and Using Notes

PROJECT

2

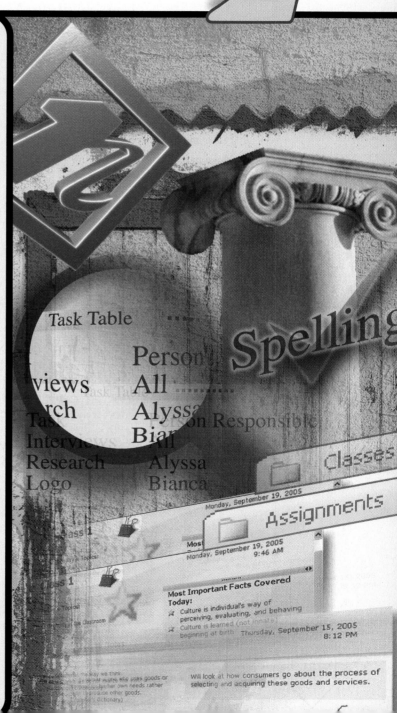

CASE PERSPECTIVE

Alyssa Ashton, a student at Penn County Community College (PCCC), uses OneNote to take notes in her classes. She is comfortable working with pages and sections in OneNote. She knows how to use containers to enter text onto her pages. She appreciates the ease with which she can format and highlight text. She has found the ability to use lists very helpful, and she especially appreciates being able to create outlines and tables quickly and easily. She takes full advantage of the capability of adding note flags to her notes.

Alyssa now wants to expand her use of OneNote. She would like to use folders to further organize her notes. She plans to create a folder called Assignments for all her various assignments. She also plans to create a folder called Classes. Alyssa anticipates adding course notes for a course in Culture and Diversity that she is taking. She will place sections for both her classes, BU 150 and ED 170, in this folder.

Once she has done so, she plans to move her existing pages to the appropriate locations in the notebook. She wants to learn the best way to navigate her way through her notebook and how to search her notes for specific text. She also wants to be able to list all her note flags in a convenient way so that she can easily locate the text that she had flagged. She finds that she occasionally needs to take a brief note that is not necessarily related to the notes that she currently is taking.

She has heard about the Side Notes feature of OneNote and feels this would give her an easy way to take such brief notes. She needs to be able to check her spelling. She also wants to easily modify the outline that she has already created, as well as to collapse the outline to show only the top levels.

As you read through this project, you will learn how to accomplish these various activities using OneNote.

MICROSOFT
Office OneNote 2003

Organizing and Using Notes

PROJECT

2

Objectives

You will have mastered the material in this project when you can:

- Understand the role of folders and sections
- Add folders
- Move and insert sections
- Move pages
- Delete, rename, and group pages
- Use stationery

- Create bulleted and numbered lists
- Search notes
- Use a note flags summary
- Add and view side notes
- Check spelling
- Update, collapse, and expand an outline

Introduction

OneNote offers several features to help you organize and use your notes. In addition to being able to place your pages into sections, you can further organize the sections into folders. In Figure 2-1, for example, the BU 150 and ED 170 sections both are contained within the Classes folder. OneNote has features that make it easy to navigate through the pages and sections. You can use stationery, which are special built-in templates, to create pages with the features you need. The page in Figure 2-1, for example, was created with a type of stationery that automatically includes a container into which you can place today's (the current day's) topics and another where you can add the most important facts covered today. Other stationery types have different features. You can select the one that is most relevant to the types of notes you will be taking.

OneNote makes it easy to add bulleted and numbered lists, to search your notes for specific text, or to find the notes you have flagged with note flags. You can take quick notes from any environment using the Side Notes feature of OneNote. You also can check spelling in your notes. You can modify the outlines you learned how to create in Project 1. You also can collapse the outlines to display only certain levels within the outline and then later expand the outline to show all levels.

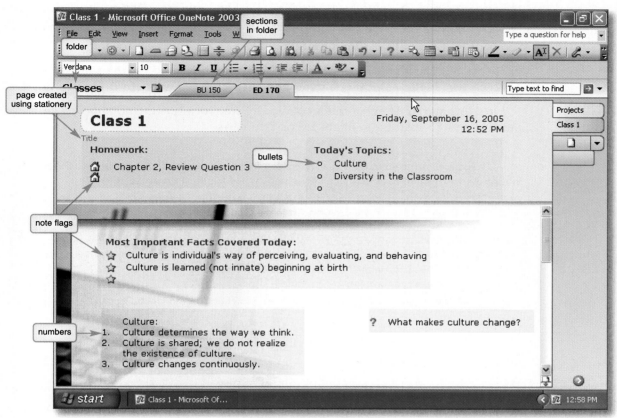

FIGURE 2-1

Project Two — Organizing and Using Notes

To illustrate the process of organizing and using notes with OneNote, this project changes the notebook organization by adding folders, moving sections between folders, moving pages between sections, and grouping pages. The project creates pages using stationery and also creates bulleted and numbered lists. It searches the notebook for specific text, and also uses a note flags summary, which is a tool that enables you to find flagged text quickly. It adds and views a side note and checks spelling. Finally, it manipulates an outline, which involves adding items to an outline, collapsing an outline, and expanding a previously collapsed outline.

Starting and Customizing OneNote

If you are stepping through this project on a computer and you want your screen to match the figures in this book, then you should change your computer's resolution to 800 × 600. For more information on how to change the resolution on your computer, see the Appendix.

More About

The OneNote Help System

Need Help? It is no further than the Type a question for help box on the menu bar in the upper-right corner of the window. Click the box that contains the text, Type a question for help (Figure 2-1), type help, and then press the ENTER key. OneNote responds with a list of topics you can click to learn more about help on any OneNote-related topic.

The following steps show how to start and customize OneNote.

To Start and Customize OneNote

1 **Click the Start button on the Windows taskbar, point to All Programs on the Start menu, and then point to Microsoft Office on the All Programs submenu.**

2 **Click Microsoft Office OneNote 2003.**

3 **If the Standard and Formatting toolbars are positioned on the same row, click the Toolbar Options button and then click Show Buttons on Two Rows.**

OneNote starts. After several seconds, OneNote displays the notebook. The Standard and Formatting toolbars are on two rows.

> **Note:** If you are instructed to use a special location for your notebook (for example, on a floppy disk in drive A), you need to perform the following steps as soon as you have started OneNote:
> 1. Click Tools on the menu bar and then click Options on the Tools menu.
> 2. Click Open and Save in the Category list in the Options dialog box.
> 3. Click My Notebook in the Paths area and then click the Modify button.
> 4. When OneNote displays the Select Folder dialog box, select the folder where the notebook will be located, click the Select button, and then click the OK button in the Options dialog box. Click the OK button in the Microsoft Office OneNote dialog box.
> 5. Quit OneNote and then restart OneNote.
>
> For details on the above steps, see the section on Notebook location in the Appendix.

Notebook Organization

More About

Moving Pages within a Section

OneNote provides a quick way to move pages within a section. Double-click the tab of the page you wish to move. Drag the page tab to the desired location in the list of pages, and then release the left mouse button.

As discussed in Project 1, the OneNote notebook is analogous to a physical notebook binder that contains tabbed section dividers. Each section contains pages, which also are tabbed for easy reference. Sometimes in a physical notebook, you may further refine the organization by placing the sections into folders that you then place in the notebook binder.

As an example, you may have three folders, the first containing three sections, the second containing four sections, and the third containing three more sections. Further, you might have a folder for class notes with a section for each class you are taking. You might have another folder for assignments. You might have still another folder for activities in which you are involved with a section for each activity. The choice of organization is up to you. You should select the folders and sections that fit your own personal preference.

This type of organization is limited in a physical notebook because of the size of the binder. You cannot keep adding folders and sections indefinitely, because you soon will run out of space. With physical notebooks, you would have to purchase another binder and start a new notebook. With OneNote, you have no such limitation. You can create as many folders and sections as you want, subject only to available disk space. Conceptually, however, the folders and sections are just like the ones you might have in your physical notebook.

In organizing your notebook, you can create folders and place sections in folders. You can even place folders within folders if you wish. For example, you could have a folder for class notes. Within this folder, a folder could be included for each semester you are in school. Within the folder for a particular semester, you could have a section for each class containing the actual notes.

Not only can you create new sections in folders, but you also can move existing sections into folders. You can move sections from one folder to another or pages from one section to another. You can delete folders, sections, or pages you no longer need.

Adding Folders

To add a folder, use the New Folder command on the Insert menu. The folder will be inserted just after the currently selected folder or section. Thus, you must make sure you have selected the correct folder or section before adding the new folder. The following steps show how to add a new folder just after the General section.

More About

Keyboard Shortcuts

Keyboard shortcuts can make it easier to move between pages and sections and to maintain organized notes. For more information, visit the OneNote 2003 More About Web page (scsite.com/one2003/more) and click Keyboard Shortcuts.

To Add a Folder

1

• **Click the tab for the General section if it is not already selected. (If the General section is not open, click File on the menu bar and then click Open on the File menu. When the File Open dialog box appears, click the General section and then click the Open button.)**

The General section is selected (Figure 2-2). Your list of sections may be different or may be in a different order.

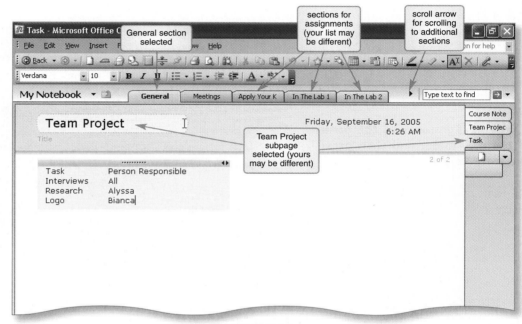

FIGURE 2-2

2

• **Click Insert on the menu bar.**

The Insert menu appears (Figure 2-3).

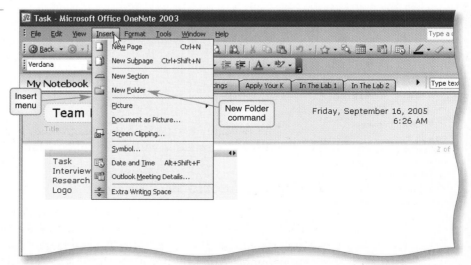

FIGURE 2-3

3

- **Click New Folder on the Insert menu.**

OneNote creates a new folder (Figure 2-4). The icon on the new tab signifies that it is a folder.

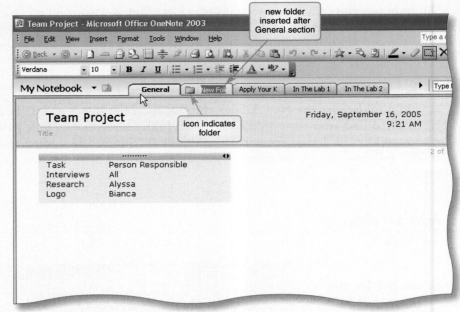

FIGURE 2-4

4

- **Type** Assignments **as the name of the new folder and then press the ENTER key.**

The name of the new folder is changed (Figure 2-5).

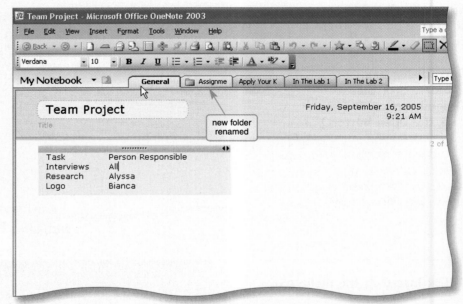

FIGURE 2-5

Other Ways

1. On File menu click New, click Folder in New task pane
2. Right-click currently selected folder or section, click New Folder on shortcut menu

The Assignments folder has been created. It currently contains no sections. You can create new sections within the folder or move sections to the folder.

Moving Sections

You can move sections into folders as well as move sections from one folder to another. The following steps show how to move the sections you created for the assignments in Project 1 to the Assignments folder. If you did not complete all the assignments, you will not have all the sections shown below.

To Move Sections

1

• **Right-click the Apply Your Knowledge section (the first section to be moved).**

The shortcut menu for the Apply Your Knowledge section appears (Figure 2-6). Your sections may not be in the same order.

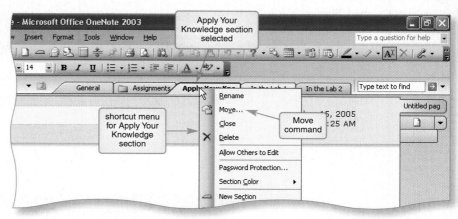

FIGURE 2-6

2

• **Click Move on the shortcut menu.**

• **When OneNote displays the Move Section To dialog box, click the Assignments folder in the Move section to list.**

The Move Section To dialog box appears (Figure 2-7). The Assignments folder is selected.

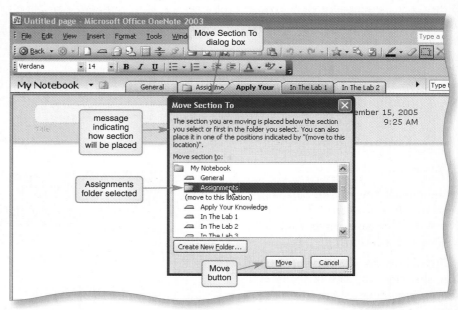

FIGURE 2-7

3

• **Click the Move button.**

The Apply Your Knowledge section is moved (Figure 2-8). It now is located in the Assignments folder.

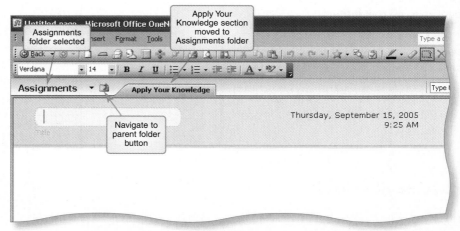

FIGURE 2-8

4

• **Click the Navigate to parent folder button (see Figure 2-8).**

The My Notebook folder, the highest level in the notebook, once again appears (Figure 2-9).

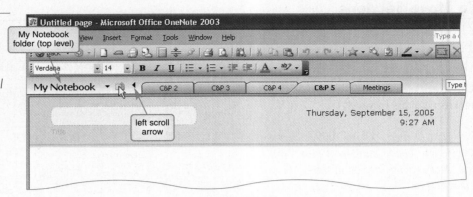

FIGURE 2-9

5

• **If the Assignments folder does not appear, as is the case in Figure 2-9, repeatedly click the left scroll arrow to return to the beginning of the list of sections and folders.**

The Assignments folder appears (Figure 2-10).

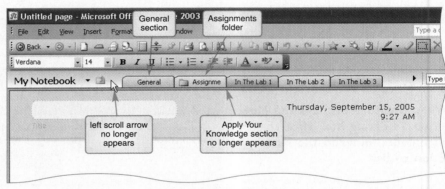

FIGURE 2-10

6

• **Right-click the In The Lab 1 section. (If you do not have an In The Lab 1 section, right-click any In The Lab section.)**

• **Click Move on the shortcut menu. If a plus sign appears in front of the Assignments folder, click the plus sign to change the plus sign to a minus sign and display the contents of the folder.**

• **Click the Apply Your Knowledge section (the most recently added section) in the Move section to list.**

The Apply Your Knowledge section is selected in the Move Section To dialog box (Figure 2-11).

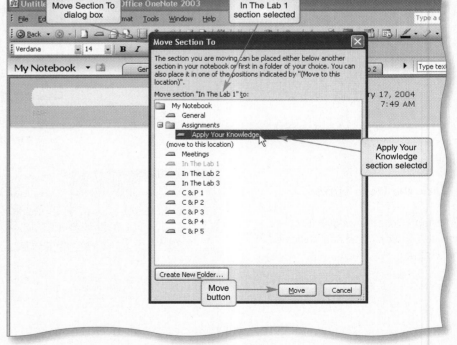

7

• **Click the Move button.**

The In The Lab 1 section is moved to the Assignments folder.

FIGURE 2-11

You now can move any remaining assignment sections to the Assignments folder. In each case, click the most recently added section in the Move Section To dialog box. For example, when adding the In The Lab 2 section, click the In The Lab 1 section. Be careful to click the section name and not the text in parentheses (move to this location) below the section name. The following steps show how to move any remaining sections to the Assignments folder.

To Move Remaining Sections

1 **Right-click the section to be moved.**

2 **Click Move on the shortcut menu.**

3 **When OneNote displays the Move Section To dialog box, click the most recently added section.**

4 **Click the Move button.**

Other Ways

1. Click Move Page To button on Standard toolbar
2. On Edit menu point to Move Page To, click Another Section on Move Page To submenu

The sections are moved to the Assignments folder. The Notebook currently contains two sections, General and Meetings, in addition to the Assignments folder (Figure 2-12).

Adding a Folder

You can add as many additional folders as you wish. The following steps show how to create an additional folder called Classes.

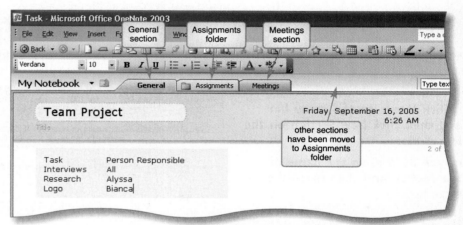

FIGURE 2-12

To Add an Additional Folder

1 **Click Insert on the menu bar and then click New Folder on the Insert menu.**

2 **Type** Classes **as the name of the new folder, and then press the ENTER key.**

The Classes folder is added to the notebook (Figure 2-13).

Inserting Sections

You can insert (create) new sections. If you wish to insert the new section in a folder, you first must select the folder. The steps on the next page show how to insert a new section in the Classes folder.

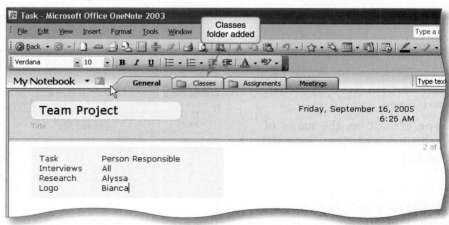

FIGURE 2-13

To Insert Sections

1

• **Click the Classes tab.**

The Classes folder is selected (Figure 2-14). Currently no sections are open in the folder.

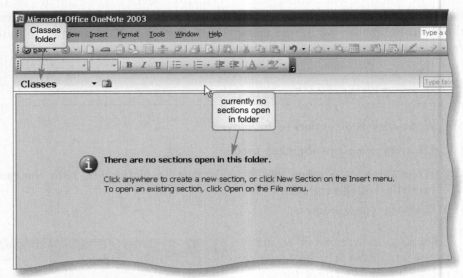

FIGURE 2-14

2

• **Click Insert on the menu bar and then click New Section on the Insert menu.**

• **Type** BU 150 **as the name of the section and then press the ENTER key.**

The BU 150 section is added to the Classes folder (Figure 2-15).

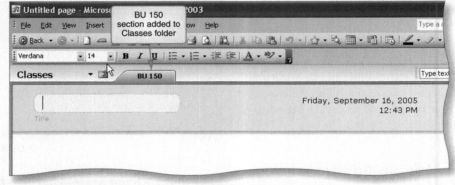

FIGURE 2-15

3

• **Click Insert on the menu bar and then click New Section on the Insert menu.**

• **Type** ED 170 **as the name of the section and then press the ENTER key.**

The ED 170 section is added to the Classes folder (Figure 2-16).

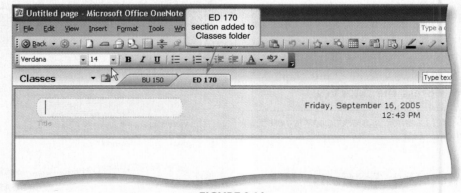

FIGURE 2-16

The Classes folder now contains two sections.

Moving Pages

As you change your notebook organization, it sometimes is necessary to move a page from one section to another. The following steps show how to move the pages that currently are in the General section to the BU 150 section in the Classes folder.

To Move Pages

1

• **Click the Navigate to parent folder button.**

• **If necessary, click the General tab to make sure the General section is selected.**

• **Right-click the Course Notes page tab and then point to Move Page To on the shortcut menu.**

The shortcut menu for the Course Notes page and the Move Page To submenu appear (Figure 2-17).

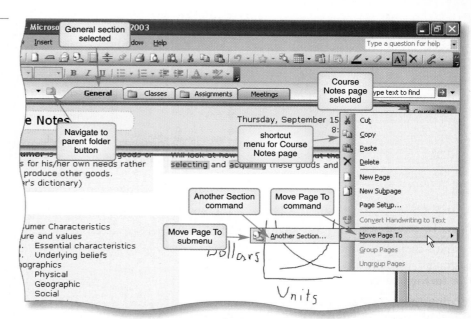

FIGURE 2-17

2

• **Click Another Section on the Move Page To submenu.**

OneNote displays the Move or Copy Pages dialog box (Figure 2-18).

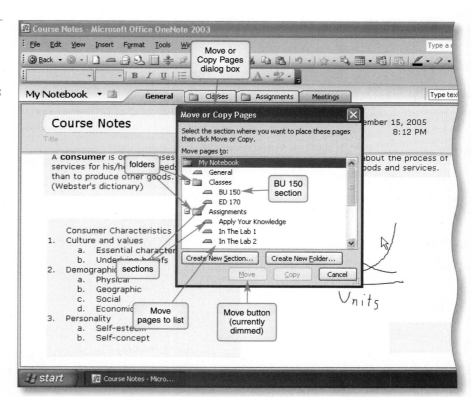

FIGURE 2-18

Microsoft Office
OneNote 2003

3

• **Click the Classes\BU 150 section in the Move or Copy Pages dialog box and then click the Move button.**

• **Right-click the Team Project page tab and then point to Move Page To on the shortcut menu.**

The page has been moved (Figure 2-19). The Move Page To submenu appears. The submenu currently contains Classes\BU 150 as one of the options.

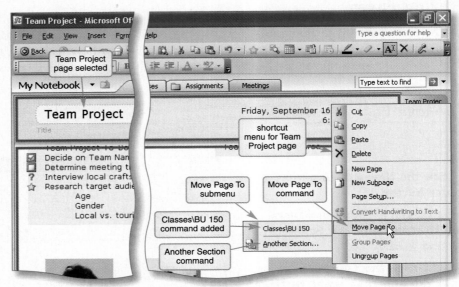

FIGURE 2-19

4

• **Click Classes\BU 150 on the Move Page To submenu.**

• **Right-click the Team Project page tab, which now is the tab for the former subpage.**

• **Point to Move Page To on the shortcut menu and then click Classes\BU 150.**

All sections now have been moved (Figure 2-20). The General Section now is empty.

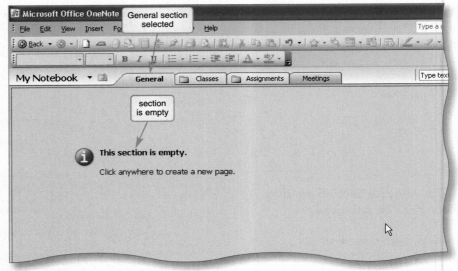

FIGURE 2-20

5

• **Click the Classes folder tab to move to the Classes folder and then click the BU 150 section tab.**

The BU 150 section is selected (Figure 2-21).

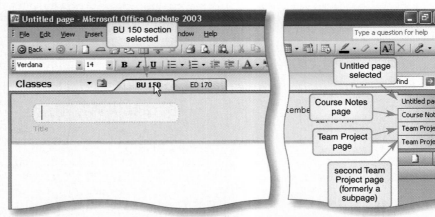

FIGURE 2-21

The BU 150 section currently contains an Untitled page, which should not be in the section. It also contains the Course Notes page, and two Team Project pages. The second Team Project page should be a subpage. Correcting these problems requires deletion of the Untitled page and making the second Team Project page a subpage of the first (called grouping, which is discussed in the next section).

Deleting a Page

You can delete any page that you do not want. For example, the Untitled page in this section is unnecessary. The following steps show how to delete the Untitled page.

To Delete a Page

1

• **Right-click the Untitled page tab.**

The shortcut menu for the Untitled page appears (Figure 2-22).

2

• **Click Delete on the shortcut menu.**

The page is removed.

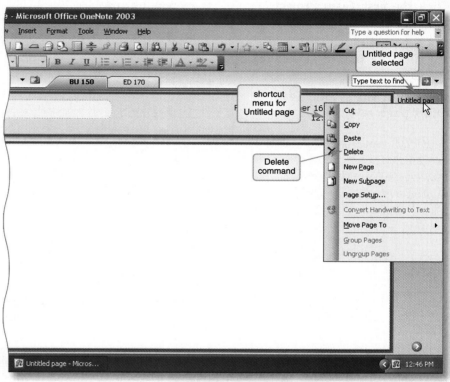

FIGURE 2-22

Deleting a page is slightly different from deleting a folder or section. When you delete a folder or section, OneNote moves the folder or section to the Windows Recycle Bin. You can use the Recycle Bin to restore the deleted folder or section if you wish, provided you have not emptied the Recycle Bin, in which case the folder or section no longer would be available. When you delete a page, however, OneNote places the deleted page in a special folder called Deleted Pages. To access the Deleted Pages folder, click the My Notebook box arrow, and then click Deleted Pages in the list of folders and sections that appears. If you wish to restore a page you have deleted, right-click the page tab for the deleted page, and then click Restore on the shortcut menu. The Deleted Pages folder is normally emptied every time you quit OneNote. If this is not acceptable, you can configure how often the Deleted pages folder is emptied. For details on how to do so, see the Appendix.

More About

Ungrouping Pages

You can ungroup pages that currently are grouped. To do so, right-click one of the page tabs for a page in the group and then click Ungroup Pages on the shortcut menu. The pages that had been grouped now will be stand-alone pages.

Grouping Pages

You can group pages when you first create them by creating subpages. To group pages that already have been created, you first need to make sure the page you want to be the main page is placed immediately before the page or pages that should be subpages. If you need to move a page to accomplish the correct order, double-click the tab of the page you need to move, and then drag the page to the desired location. Once the pages are in the correct order, select the main page and all the subpages, and then use the Group Pages command as illustrated in the following steps.

To Group Pages

1

• **Click the first Team Project page tab.**

• **Hold down the SHIFT key and then click the second Team Project page tab.**

• **Right-click the second Team Project page tab.**

The shortcut menu appears (Figure 2-23). If Group Pages is dimmed on the shortcut menu, you did not click the tabs correctly and will need to repeat Step 1.

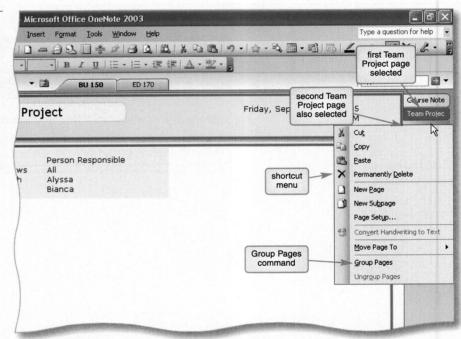

FIGURE 2-23

2

• **Click Group Pages on the shortcut menu.**

The second Team Project page is once again a subpage (Figure 2-24).

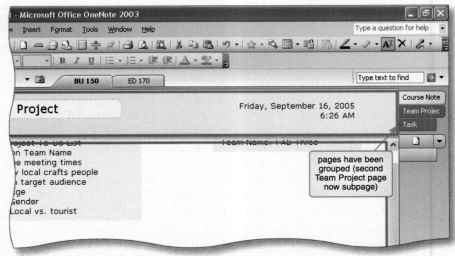

FIGURE 2-24

Other Ways

1. Select pages, on Edit menu click Group Pages

Navigating in the Notebook

You already have seen some of the key methods of navigating in the notebook. You can move to a folder by clicking the folder's tab. Similarly, you can move to a section by clicking the section's tab. Once in a section, you can move to a page by clicking the page's tab. Figure 2-25 illustrates other tools for navigating.

More About

Moving or Copying Grouped Pages

It is possible to keep grouped pages together when moving or copying. To do so, double-click the first page in the group and then SHIFT-click the other pages in the group. You then can move or copy the pages just as you would individual pages. In the process, the pages still will be grouped when the operation is complete.

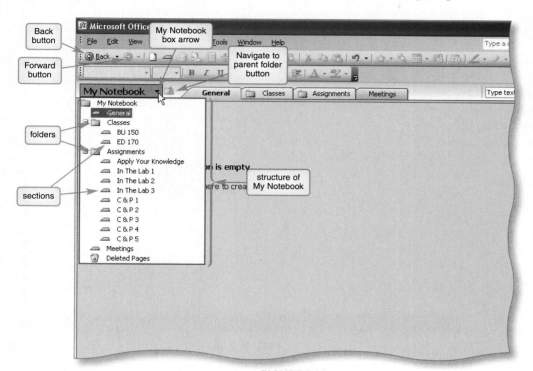

FIGURE 2-25

To move from a folder back to its parent folder, click the Navigate to parent folder button. After you have visited several pages and want to retrace your steps, that is, move backwards through the pages you visited, repeatedly click the Back button. If you are moving backward and want to move forward again through the list of visited pages, click the Forward button. Both buttons contain arrows that you can click to display a list of recently visited pages. To select any page in the list, simply click the page.

If you click the My Notebook box arrow, you will see all the folders and sections in the notebook. To move to a folder or section, simply click it in the list. Even if you do not use this list to navigate, you still may find it useful for viewing the entire structure of your notebook in an organized fashion.

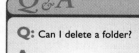

Q: Can I delete a folder?

A: Yes. To delete a folder, right-click the folder tab and then click Delete on the shortcut menu.

Using Stationery

OneNote contains several templates, called **stationery**, that you can use when creating new pages. The various stationery types come predesigned with appropriate note containers, note flags, and lists to make note taking easier. These stationery types are organized in categories such as Planners, Decorative, Business, and Academic. To use stationery, you should select the particular stationery type that will be most useful for the notes you are about to take. The steps on the next page show how to create a new page based on whatever stationery type you want. The steps use the Simple Lecture Notes stationery type, which is found in the Academic category.

To Use Stationery

1

• **If necessary, click the Classes folder and then click the ED 170 section.**

• **Click the New Page From Stationery arrow.**

A list of recently selected stationery choices appears (Figure 2-26). (Your list will probably be different.) At the bottom of the list is More Stationery Choices and Options.

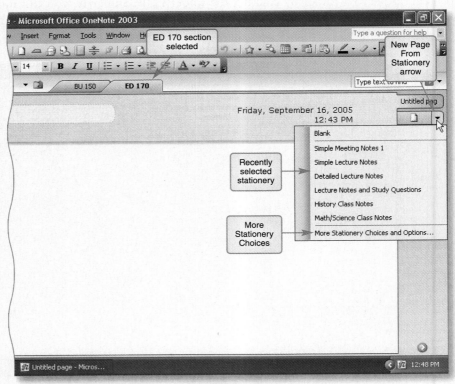

FIGURE 2-26

2

• **Click More Stationery Choices and Options. (If your list contains Simple Lecture Notes, like the list in the figure, you could click it at this time and skip Steps 3 and 4.)**

The Stationery task pane appears (Figure 2-27). Your stationery list may be in a different order.

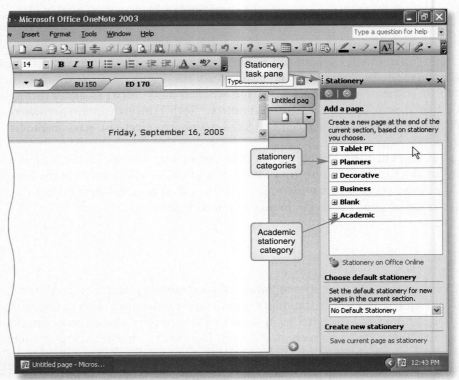

FIGURE 2-27

3

• **Click the plus sign in front of the Academic category.**

The stationery choices in the Academic stationery category appear (Figure 2-28).

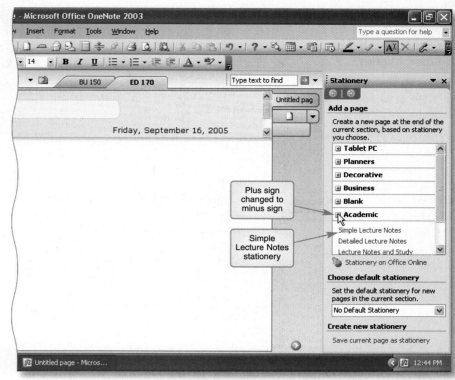

FIGURE 2-28

4

• **Click the Simple Lecture Notes link.**

OneNote creates a new page using the Simple Lecture Notes stationery (Figure 2-29).

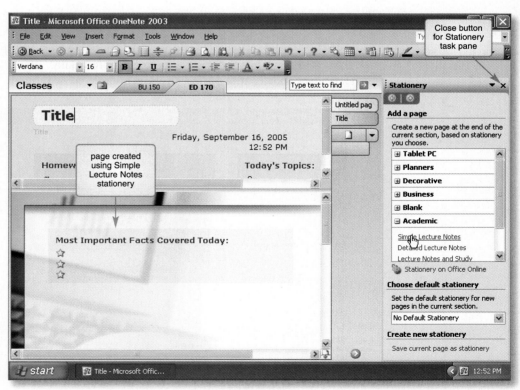

FIGURE 2-29

5

• **Close the Stationery task pane by clicking its Close button.**

• **Erase the word Title in the title area for the page.**

• **Type** Class 1 **as the title of the page.**

The Class 1 page is created using the Simple Lecture Notes stationery (Figure 2-30). The task pane no longer appears.

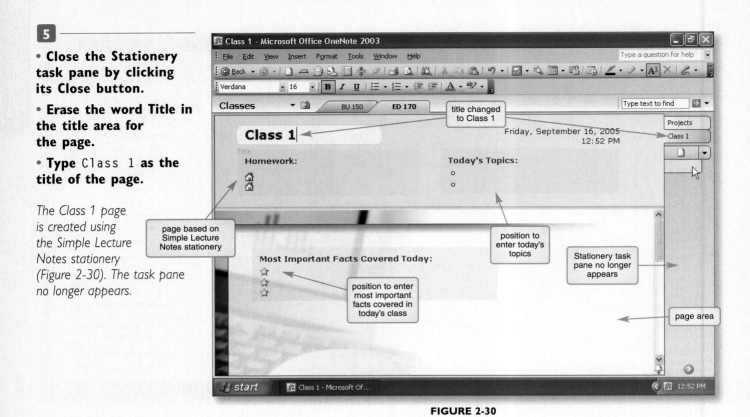

FIGURE 2-30

Many other types of stationery are available that set up your pages with organized areas and headings for specific types of note-taking. Figure 2-31 shows another type of stationery that is appropriate in an academic environment.

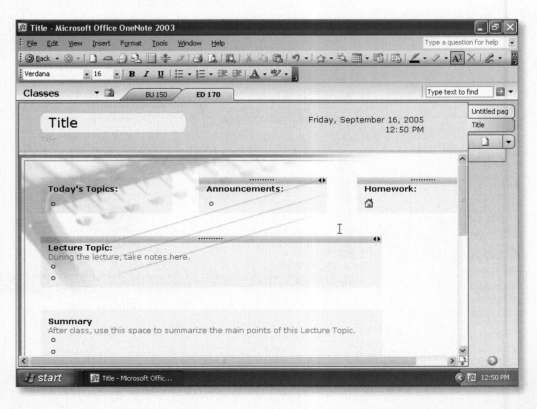

FIGURE 2-31

Figure 2-32 shows yet another type of stationery for an academic environment.

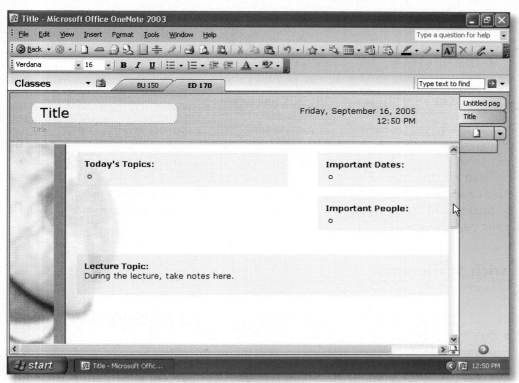

FIGURE 2-32

Figure 2-33 shows a type of stationery that would be appropriate for taking notes at a business meeting.

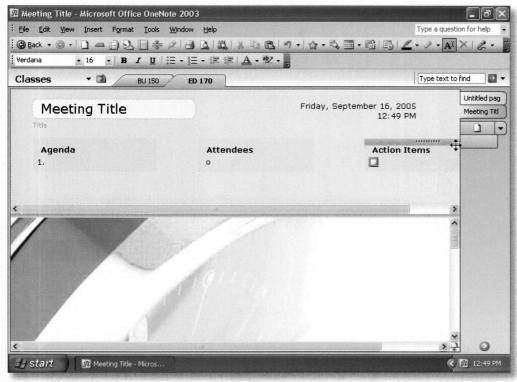

FIGURE 2-33

This is a small sample of the types of stationery that are available. You should select the one that is most suitable for the particular type of notes you will be taking. In addition, you can create custom stationery based on one of your own pages of notes by selecting the page, and then clicking Save current page as stationery in the Stationery task pane. You then can use this stationery in the future just like any of the other stationery types.

Using a Page Created with Stationery

To use a page created with stationery, simply fill in the sections appropriately. In the page shown in Figure 2-30 on page ONE 82, for example, you would enter today's topics in the Today's Topics container. The topics automatically would take the form of a bulleted list. You would enter important topics in the Most Important Facts Covered Today container. Each would be preceded automatically by an Important note flag. You then would enter your notes in the page area. The following steps show how to use the page shown in Figure 2-30.

To Use a Page Created with Stationery

1

• **Click after the first bullet in the Today's Topics container.**

An insertion point appears after the bullet (Figure 2-34).

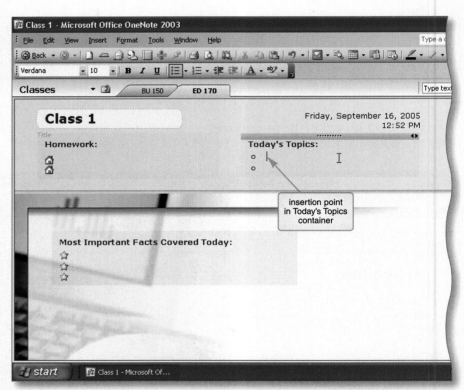

FIGURE 2-34

2

• **Type** Culture **after the bullet, press the ENTER key, and then type** Diversity in the Classroom **after the second bullet.**

Today's topics are entered (Figure 2-35).

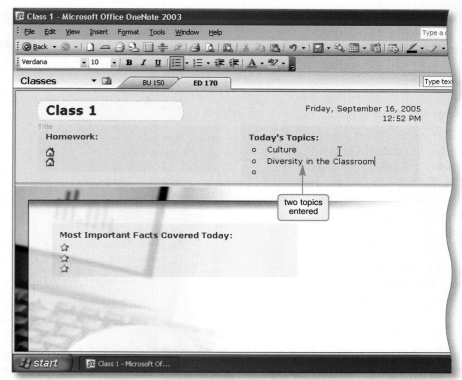

FIGURE 2-35

3

• **Click after the first note flag below Most Important Facts Covered Today.**

• **Type** Culture is individual's way of perceiving, evaluating, and behaving **after the note flag.**

The first important fact is entered (Figure 2-36).

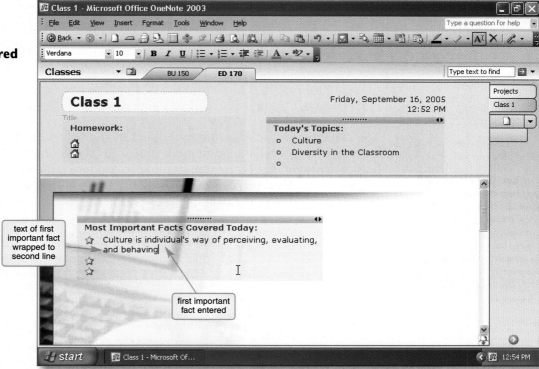

FIGURE 2-36

4

• **Click after the second note flag, and then type** Culture is learned (not innate) beginning at birth **after the note flag.**

• **Resize the Most Important Fact Covered Today container so that the first fact appears on one line and move the container to the approximate position shown in Figure 2-37.**

• **Click after the first note flag below Homework and type** Chapter 2, Review Question 3 **as shown in the figure.**

• **Click below the Most Important Facts Covered Today container, type** Culture: **in a new container, and then press the ENTER key to create the additional container shown in the figure.**

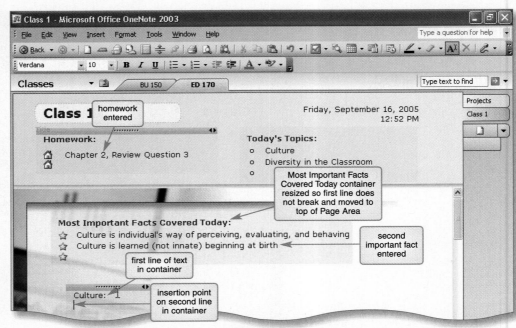

FIGURE 2-37

The most important facts covered today and the homework assignment have been entered. A container has been created in the body of the page.

Bulleted and Numbered Lists

You can create bulleted or numbered lists in your notes. In the process, you can select from a variety of bullet and number styles. To create a bulleted list, use the Bullets button arrow on the Formatting toolbar to produce a menu of available bullet styles (Figure 2-38). You then can select the desired style. If the style you want is not one of the five appearing in the menu, you can select More to choose from additional styles.

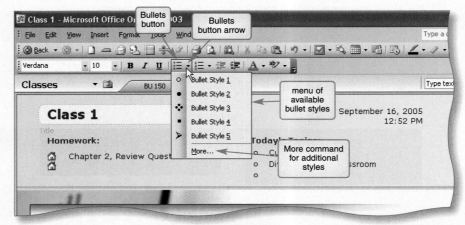

FIGURE 2-38

To create a numbered list, use the Numbering button arrow on the Formatting toolbar to produce a menu of available numbering styles (Figure 2-39). You then can select the desired style. If the style you want is not one of the five appearing in the menu, you can select More to choose from additional styles.

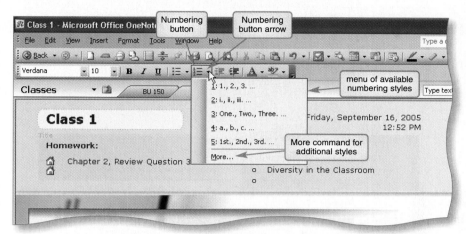

FIGURE 2-39

Creating a Numbered List

The following steps illustrate creating a numbered list using the Numbering button arrow on the Standard toolbar. If the type of numbering you want to use appears on the face of the Numbering button, you simply could click the button. It is good practice, however, to click the button arrow and then select the desired type from the menu. Using that process ensures that you always get the numbering type you want.

More About

Outline Settings

You can customize both the distance that OneNote indents items in your outline and the spacing between items. To change these settings, click Format on the menu bar and then click List on the Format menu. In the List task pane, select the desired indent (Horizontal spacing) or spacing between items (Vertical spacing).

To Create a Numbered List

1

• **Click the Numbering button arrow (see Figure 2-39) and then click the first numbering style in the menu of available numbering styles.**

• **Type** Culture determines the way we think. **as the first item in the list.**

OneNote creates a numbered list (Figure 2-40). The first item in the list is entered.

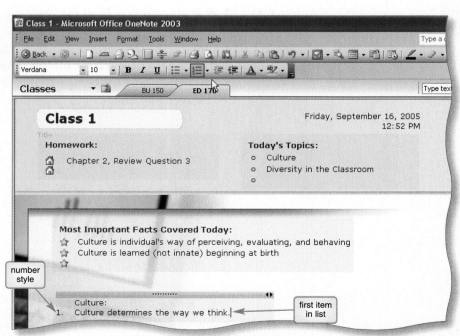

FIGURE 2-40

2

• **Press the ENTER key, type**
Culture is shared; we do not
realize the existence of
culture. **as the second entry,
and then press the ENTER key.**

*When you press the ENTER key, OneNote
automatically places the number 2 at the
left margin of the next line in preparation
for the entry of the second list item.*

3

• **Type** Culture changes
continuously. **as the
third entry. Resize the container
to the approximate size shown in
Figure 2-41.**

*The list is complete and the container is
resized (Figure 2-14). The resized
container allows room to enter a question
next to the container.*

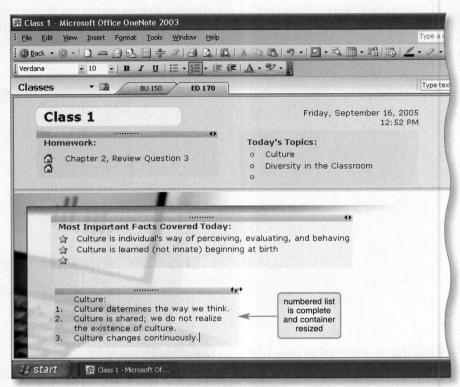

FIGURE 2-41

OneNote has numbered the list automatically according to the selected
numbering style.

Adding Containers and Note Flags

To add a container, type the desired text in the container. If you want to add a note
flag, be sure the insertion point is positioned somewhere within the text to be
flagged. The following steps show how to add containers and note flags.

To Add a Container and Note Flag

1

• **Click to the right of the numbered list, far enough away to create a separate container, and then type** What makes culture change? **in the container.**

• **Click the Note Flag button arrow on the Standard toolbar.**

The menu of available note flags appears (Figure 2-42).

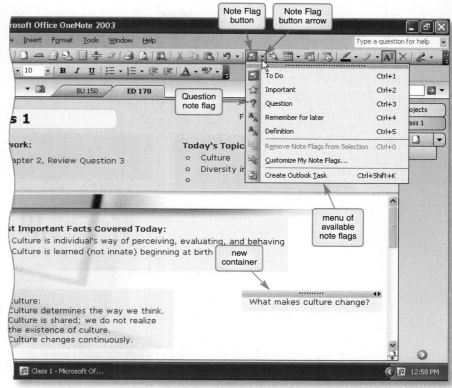

FIGURE 2-42

2

• **Click the Question note flag.**

OneNote adds a Question note flag (Figure 2-43).

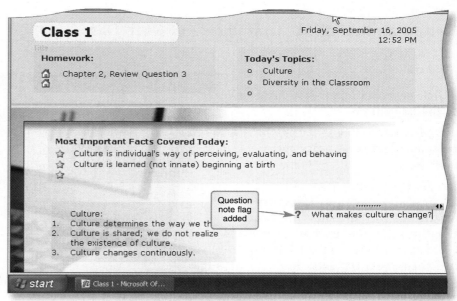

FIGURE 2-43

Renaming a Page

If you do not enter a title for a page, the page name is Untitled. You can rename a page by adding a page title. The following step renames the Untitled page.

To Rename a Page

1

• **Click the Untitled page tab to select it.**

• **If necessary, click the title area for the page, and then type** Projects **as the name.**

The name of the Untitled page is changed to Projects (Figure 2-44).

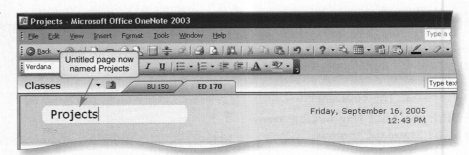

FIGURE 2-44

This process effectively removed the Untitled page and added a page titled Projects. You could have achieved the same result by first deleting the Untitled page and then adding the Projects page.

Add an Additional Container and Note Flags

To add a container, type the desired text in the container. If you want to add note flags to a paragraph within the container, be sure the insertion point is positioned somewhere within the paragraph before clicking the Note Flag button arrow. The following step illustrates adding a container and then adding note flags to two of the paragraphs within the container.

To Add an Additional Container and Note Flags

1

• **Click near the upper-left corner of the page area.**

• **Type** 2 Team Projects **in the container and then press the ENTER key.**

• **Press the TAB key, type** Need to determine topics **as the entry on the second line, click the Note Flag button arrow on the Standard toolbar, click the To Do note flag, and then press the ENTER key.**

• **Type** Need to make schedules **as the entry on the third line and then click the Note Flag button on the Standard toolbar.**

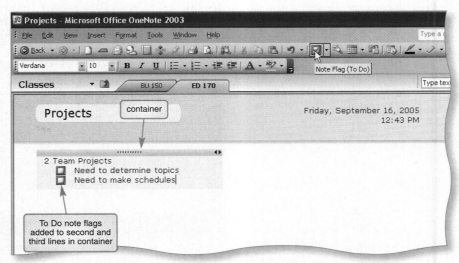

FIGURE 2-45

The text and note flags appear on the page (Figure 2-45). Because the type of note flag you want to use appears on the face of the Note Flag button, you need only to click the button rather than the button arrow.

Searching in the Notebook

You easily can search your notes for a particular word or phrase. To do so, you use the Type text to find box above the page tabs. Once your search is completed, you can move to the beginning of the search item list by repeatedly clicking the Previous Match button. You can then easily step through the items that matched your search. The following steps illustrate searching in the notebook.

To Search Notes

1

• **Click in the Type text to find box and then type** Team Project **(Figure 2-46).**

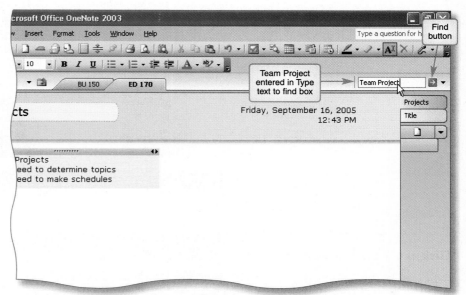

FIGURE 2-46

2

• **Click the Find button.**

• **If necessary, repeatedly click the Previous Match button (the left arrow) to move to the first item (1 of 4).**

OneNote finds and highlights the first item containing the search text (Figure 2-47). The Type text to find box is replaced by the search text, and an indication of the number of matches of the search text that were found and the relative position in the list of matches. The currently highlighted text is the first of four matches. The Previous Match (left arrow) and Next Match (right arrow) buttons allow you to move between the matches of the search text. The number of matches may vary.

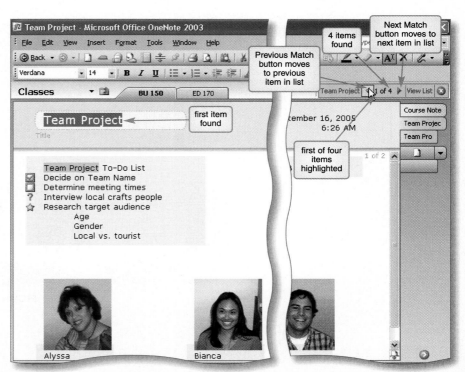

FIGURE 2-47

3

• **Click the Next Match button.**

The next match is highlighted (Figure 2-48).

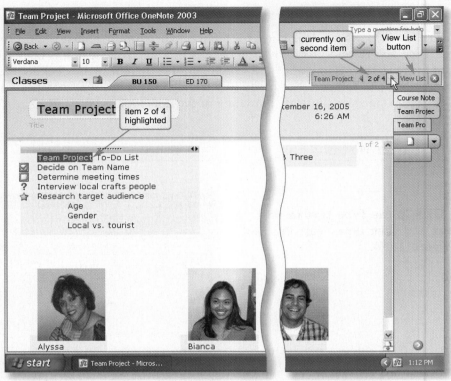

FIGURE 2-48

4

• **Click the View List button.**

The Page List task pane appears containing all matches (Figure 2-49).

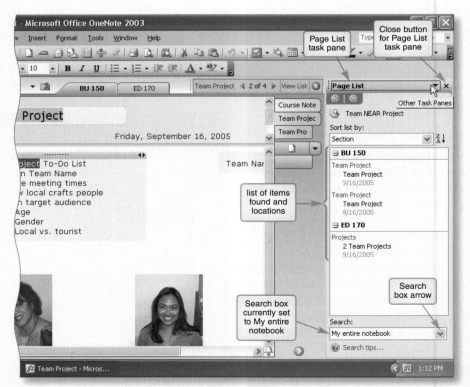

FIGURE 2-49

5

• **Close the task pane by clicking its Close button.**

The task pane no longer appears (Figure 2-50).

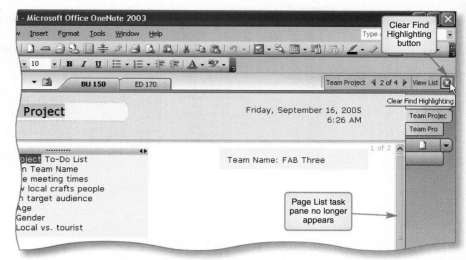

FIGURE 2-50

6

• **Click the Clear Find Highlighting button.**

The Find highlighting box no longer appears (Figure 2-51). OneNote once again displays the Type text to find box.

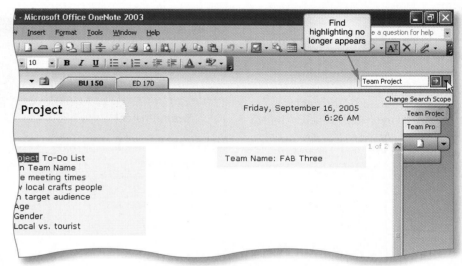

FIGURE 2-51

If you wish, you can change the scope of the search by clicking the Search box arrow (see Figure 2-49), and then selecting the desired entry in the list. As soon as you make your selection, OneNote will rerun the search and update the page list accordingly.

Using a Note Flags Summary

Note flags make it easy to discern the paragraphs with which the flags are associated whenever you look through your notes. An added benefit is that they provide another convenient way to search through your notes. You can list the note flags in a **note flags summary**. The summary shows each note flag along with the corresponding text. You can organize the summary in a variety of ways. The following steps show how to create a note flags summary.

Other Ways

1. On Edit menu click Find
2. Press CTRL+F

More About

Using Note Flags Summary to Jump to a Flag

You can use the Note Flags Summary task pane to move directly to the page and section that contains a flagged note. To do so, simply click the desired note flag.

To View a Note Flags Summary

1

• **Click View on the menu bar.**

The View menu appears (Figure 2-52).

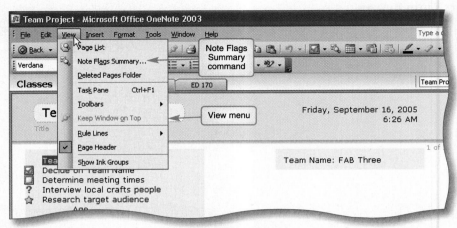

FIGURE 2-52

2

• **Click Note Flags Summary on the View menu.**

The Note Flags Summary task pane appears (Figure 2-53). The summary comprises all the notes marked with note flags in each section so you easily can refer to information that you want to follow up on or remember.

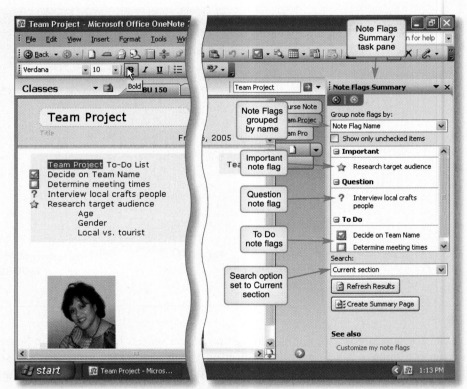

FIGURE 2-53

Other Ways

1. Click Note Flags Summary button on Standard toolbar

You can change the scope of the search by clicking the Search box arrow (Figure 2-54), and then selecting the desired entry in the list. Current section indicates that only note flags in the currently selected section should be included in this list. Current folder would include all note flags in the current folder, thus showing note flags in both the BU 150 and ED 170 sections. A variety of other options are available as well.

You also can change the way note flags are grouped by clicking the Group note flags by box arrow (Figure 2-55). You then can select the desired grouping, and OneNote will rearrange the note flags in the Note Flags Summary accordingly.

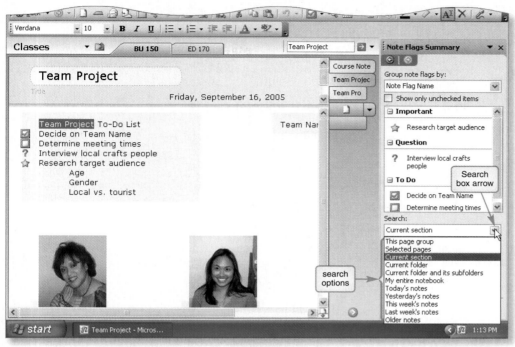

FIGURE 2-54

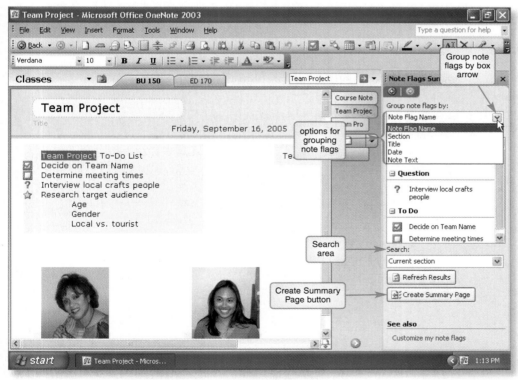

FIGURE 2-55

Creating a Note Flags Summary Page

If you want to print a list of your note flags, you can place the list on a special page, called a note flags summary page. You then can print that page. The steps on the next page show how to create a note flags summary page. The steps print the page and then delete it.

To Create and Print a Note Flags Summary Page

1

• **Click the Create Summary Page button in the Search area in the Note Flags Summary task pane (see Figure 2-55 on the previous page).**

• **Click the Close button in the Note Flags Summary task pane.**

A Note Flags summary page is added to the current section (Figure 2-56). The title of your page may be different.

2

• **Click the Print button on the Standard toolbar to print the page (see Figure 2-56).**

OneNote prints the note flags summary page.

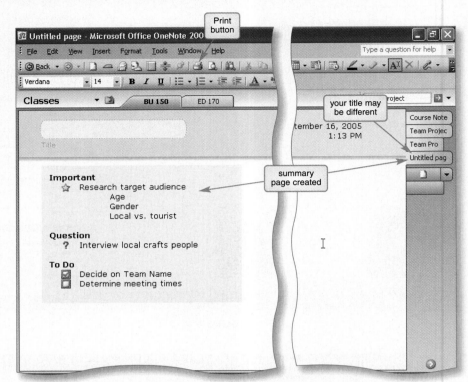

FIGURE 2-56

3

• **Delete the note flags summary page by right-clicking its page tab and then clicking Delete on the shortcut menu.**

• **Click the Team Project page tab.**

The page no longer appears (Figure 2-57).

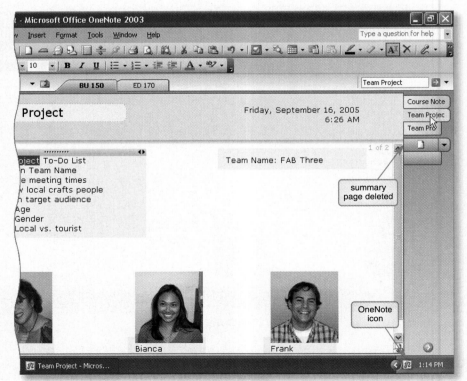

FIGURE 2-57

Usually after printing the note flags summary page, you will not need it any further, so you will delete it as in the previous steps, although it is not necessary to do so. You can keep it as another page in your notebook for as long as you like. You need to be aware that the page is not updated; that is, if you add additional note flags, they will not be reflected in the note flags summary page. You would need to recreate the page in order for the additional note flags to be included.

More About

Removing Note Flags

You can remove a note flag you no longer need. To do so, right-click the note flag and then click Remove Note Flag on the shortcut menu.

Taking Side Notes

Sometimes when you are taking notes on a particular subject, another idea may occur to you. You may want to take a quick note, but it is not appropriate to put it on the page on which you are currently working. In such a case, you can create a **side note**. Side notes are placed in a special side note section. You also can take side notes while working in other applications, as long as the OneNote icon appears in the notification area of the Windows taskbar. (If the OneNote icon does not appear in the notification area, the Place OneNote icon in notification area of taskbar check box is not checked. For details on this check box, see the Other options section of the Appendix.) The following steps show how to take a side note.

To Take a Side Note

1

• **Click the OneNote icon in the notification area of the Windows taskbar (see Figure 2-57). (If the OneNote icon does not appear in the notification area, click Window on the menu bar and then click New Side Note Window.)**

A Side Note window opens (Figure 2-58).

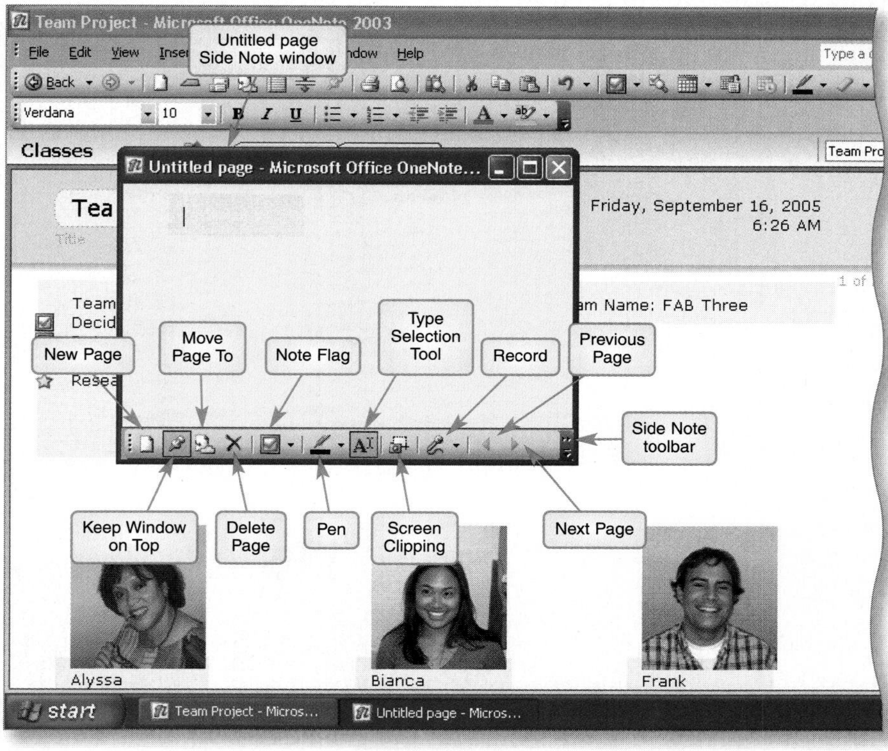

FIGURE 2-58

2

• **Click in the Side Note window and then type** Need to check on schedule for next semester ASAP **in the window.**

The side note is entered (Figure 2-59).

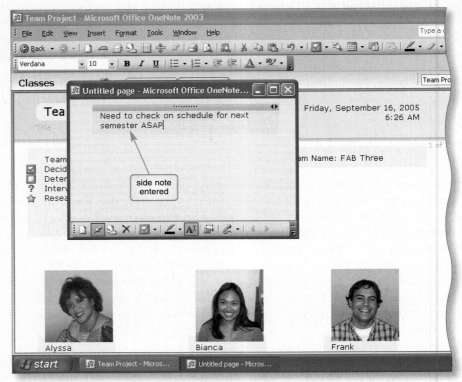

FIGURE 2-59

3

• **Click the Note Flag button arrow on the Side Note toolbar.**

The menu of available note flags appears (Figure 2-60).

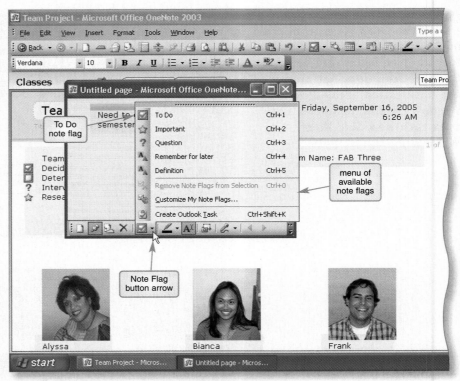

FIGURE 2-60

4

• **Click the To Do note flag.**

A To Do note flag is added to the side note (Figure 2-61).

5

• **Close the Side Note window by clicking its Close button.**

The side note window is closed. The side note has been stored.

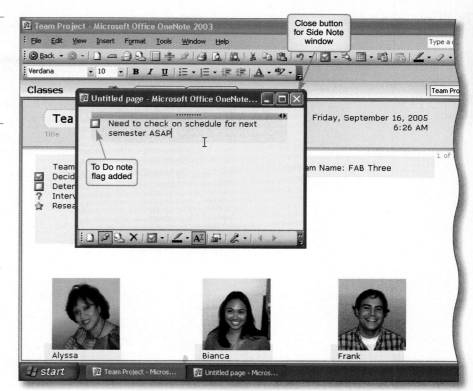

FIGURE 2-61

Other Ways

1. On Window menu click New Side Note Window
2. Press CTRL+SHIFT+M

You do not have to be working in OneNote to take side notes. You can take them from other applications using exactly the same process. Click the OneNote icon in the notification area of the Windows taskbar and then take the side note. Close the Side Note window when you are done.

Two buttons on the Side Note toolbar are especially useful when working with side notes: the Previous Page button and the Keep Window on Top button (see Figure 2-58 on page ONE 97). If you want to move to a previous side note, click the Previous Page button on the Side Note toolbar. Normally, when you create a side note, the Keep Window on Top button is selected. This means the Side Note window will remain visible as you move from page to page. If you would rather not have it remain visible, click the Keep Window on Top button so that it no longer is selected.

Viewing Side Notes

Side notes are stored as pages in a special section called Side Notes. OneNote creates this section automatically when you create your first side note. You can view side notes just like you view any other pages. The steps on the next page show how to view the side note created in the previous steps.

To View Side Notes

1

• **Click the Navigate to parent folder button to return to the top level.**

The Side Notes section has been added to the notebook (Figure 2-62). Your folders and sections may be in a different order.

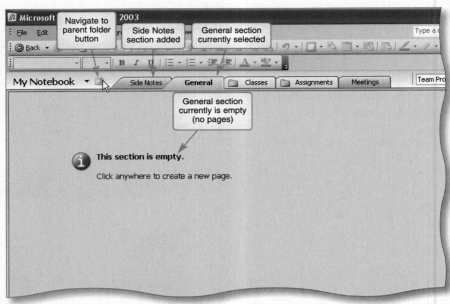

FIGURE 2-62

2

• **Click the Side Notes tab.**

The Side Notes section is selected (Figure 2-63). Only one page currently exists, because you have taken only one side note. By default, the page header does not appear. The page title contains text from the first line of the note. Your page title may be different.

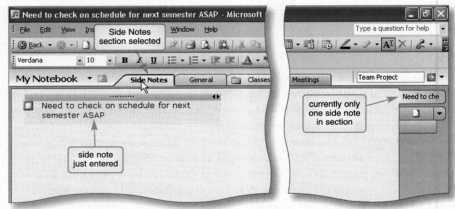

FIGURE 2-63

Once you have taken more than one side note, more than one page will be added in this section. This section behaves just like any other. You can select any page within this section by clicking its tab. You also can print a single page or print all the pages within the section (see page ONE 47 in Project 1 for information on printing pages.)

Checking Spelling

You can have OneNote check your spelling by using the Spelling command on the Tools menu (Figure 2-64). The following steps show how to use the Spelling command. (If you prefer to have OneNote check your spelling as you type, see the Appendix for details on how to configure OneNote appropriately.)

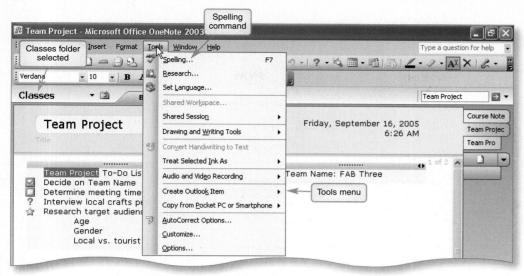

FIGURE 2-64

TO CHECK SPELLING

1. Click the Classes folder to select it, and then click Tools on the menu bar.
2. Click Spelling on the Tools menu.

Other Ways

1. Press F7

OneNote then will check your spelling. If it finds a misspelled word, it will highlight the word in the page (Figure 2-65). It also will indicate the error and offer suggestions in the Spelling task pane. You then can click the Ignore button in the Spelling task pane to ignore the error, or click the Add to Dictionary button to add the word to the dictionary so it will be accepted the next time you check spelling. To replace the word with one of the suggestions, you can click the desired suggestion to select it, and then click the Change button.

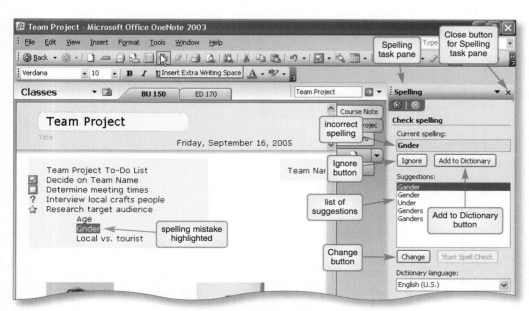

FIGURE 2-65

Once the spelling check is complete, OneNote will display the message shown in Figure 2-66 on the next page. To complete the process, click the OK button and then close the Spelling task pane.

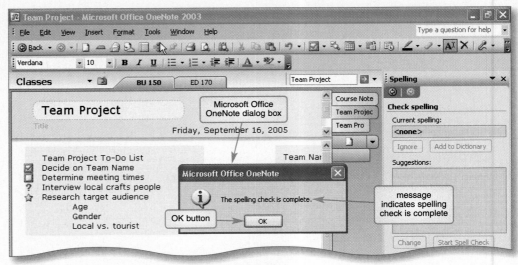

FIGURE 2-66

Modifying an Outline

You can modify an existing outline in the same fashion you originally created the outline. When you insert a new line, it automatically is placed at the same level as the previous line. To change the level, you press the TAB key to demote the item to a lower level or the BACKSPACE key to promote the item to a higher level. The following steps show how to modify an outline.

To Modify an Outline

1

• **Select the BU 150 section and the Course Notes page.**

• **Click after the word, beliefs, in 1b of the outline.**

• **Press the ENTER key.**

OneNote adds another line in the Culture and values section (Figure 2-67).

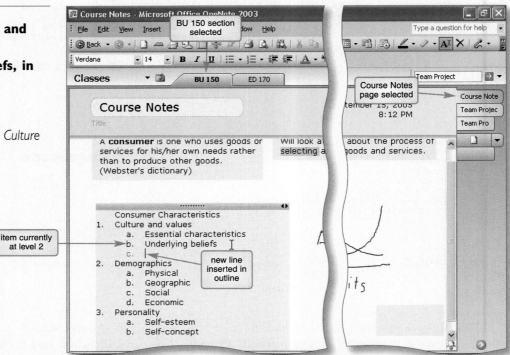

FIGURE 2-67

2

• **Press the TAB key.**

OneNote demotes the entry and indents the line appropriately for its position in the outline (Figure 2-68).

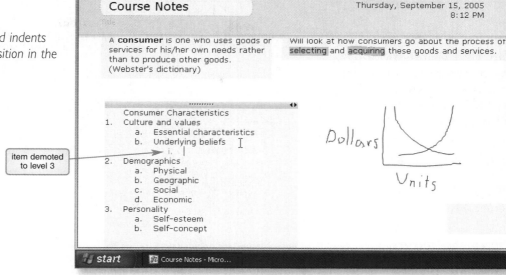

FIGURE 2-68

3

• **Type** Family **as the entry, press the ENTER key, and then type** External **as the next entry.**

OneNote indents the numbers and the entries appropriately for their positions in the outline (Figure 2-69).

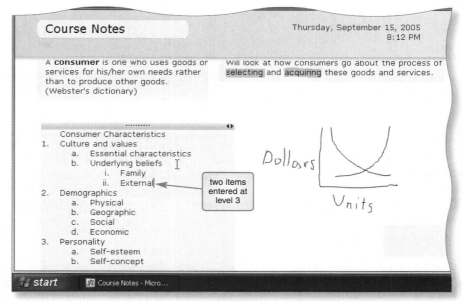

FIGURE 2-69

The outline now is complete.

Collapsing and Expanding an Outline

Outlines often contain many levels. Sometimes you may want to hide some of the lower levels so it is easier to view only the broader points in the outline. This process is called **collapsing an outline**. To later restore the complete outline is called **expanding the outline**. The steps on the next page show how to collapse and then later expand an outline. To collapse and expand an outline requires using the Outlining toolbar.

More About

Adding Body Text to an Outline

Sometimes, you may want to add text that does not follow the outline structure in the middle of an outline. Such text is called body text. To add body text, use the Outlining toolbar.

To Collapse and Expand an Outline

1

• **Click View on the menu bar, point to Toolbars on the View menu, and then click Outlining unless it is already checked on the Toolbars submenu.**

• **Click the Collapse button arrow on the Outlining toolbar.**

The Outlining toolbar appears (Figure 2-70). The Collapse button menu also appears.

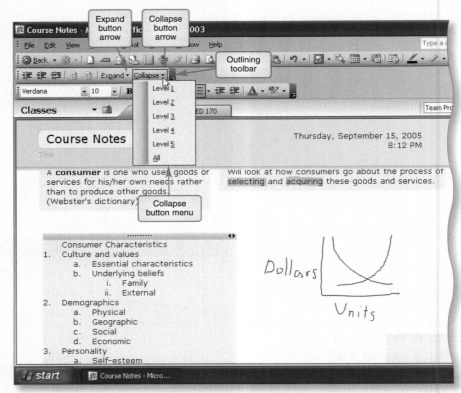

FIGURE 2-70

2

• **Click Level 2 on the Collapse button menu.**

Levels below level 2 no longer appear in the outline (Figure 2-71). In this case, only level 3 entries were hidden.

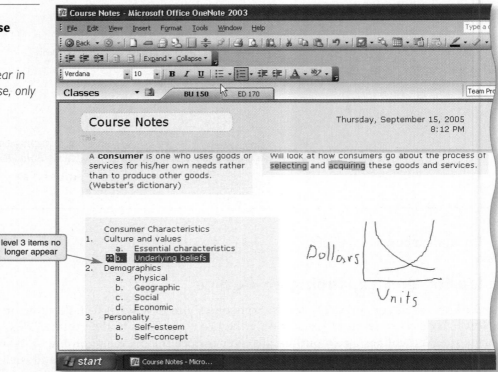

FIGURE 2-71

3

• **Click the Expand button arrow on the Outlining toolbar, and then click All on the Expand button menu.**

The entire outline once again appears (Figure 2-72).

4

• **Click View on the menu bar, point to Toolbars on the View menu, and then click Outlining to remove the check mark.**

The Outlining toolbar no longer appears.

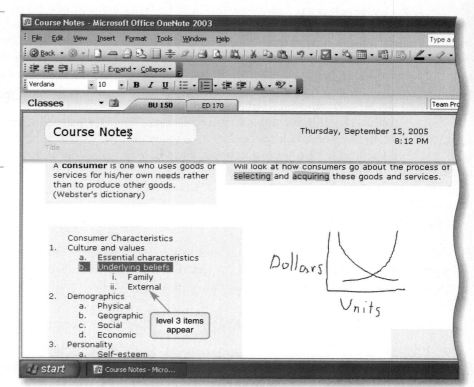

FIGURE 2-72

On some occasions while working with outlines, you might want to take the same action on all items at a particular level in an outline. To do so, click Edit on the menu bar, click Select on the Edit menu, and then select the desired level. You then can drag this text to a new position, cut or copy the text, or apply formatting to this text. Any action you take will apply to all the selected items.

If you decide that you prefer the text you originally entered as an outline to be text only, you can make this change. To do so, select the portion of the outline that now should be text and click the Make Body Text button on the Outlining toolbar.

Quitting OneNote

After you make all the changes to the notebook, Project 2 is complete and you are ready to quit OneNote. The following step shows how to quit OneNote.

To Quit OneNote

1 **Click the Close button on the OneNote title bar.**

Project Summary

In making the changes to the notebook in this project, you expanded your knowledge of OneNote. First, you were introduced to the role of folders in the notebook. You learned how to create folders, move sections to folders, and how to move pages. You also saw how to group pages that had already been created. You learned ways to navigate within the notebook. You also learned how to use stationery and saw some of the various stationery types. You learned how to create bulleted and numbered lists.

You learned to search your notes for specific text. You also learned how to create a note flags summary that enabled you to locate notes you had previously flagged. You learned how to create and use side notes. You saw how to check spelling within your notebook. Finally, you added items to an outline, collapsed an outline, and expanded an outline that you previously had collapsed.

What You Should Know

Having completed this project, you now should be able to perform the tasks below. The tasks are listed in the same order they were presented in this project. For a list of the buttons, menus, toolbars, and commands introduced in this project, see the Quick Reference Summary at the back of this book, and refer to the Page Number column.

1. Start and Customize OneNote (ONE 68)
2. Add a Folder (ONE 69)
3. Move Sections (ONE 71)
4. Move Remaining Sections (ONE 73)
5. Add an Additional Folder (ONE 73)
6. Insert Sections (ONE 74)
7. Move Pages (ONE 75)
8. Delete a Page (ONE 77)
9. Group Pages (ONE 78)
10. Use Stationery (ONE 80)
11. Use a Page Created with Stationery (ONE 84)
12. Create a Numbered List (ONE 87)
13. Add a Container and Note Flag (ONE 89)
14. Rename a Page (ONE 90)
15. Add an Additional Container and Note Flags (ONE 90)
16. Search Notes (ONE 91)
17. View a Note Flags Summary (ONE 94)
18. Create and Print a Note Flags Summary Page (ONE 96)
19. Take a Side Note (ONE 97)
20. View Side Notes (ONE 100)
21. Check Spelling (ONE 101)
22. Modify an Outline (ONE 102)
23. Collapse and Expand an Outline (ONE 104)
24. Quit OneNote (ONE 105)

Learn It Online

Instructions: To complete the Learn It Online exercises, start your browser, click the Address bar, and then enter the Web address scsite.com/one2003/learn. When the OneNote 2003 Learn It Online page is displayed, follow the instructions in the exercises below. Each exercise has instructions for printing your results, either for your own records or for submission to your instructor.

1 Project Reinforcement TF, MC, and SA

Below OneNote Project 2, click the Project Reinforcement link. Print the quiz by clicking Print on the File menu. Answer each question.

2 Flash Cards

Below OneNote Project 2, click the Flash Cards link and read the instructions. Type 20 (or a number specified by your instructor) in the Number of playing cards text box, type your name in the Enter your Name text box, and then click the Flip Card button. When the flash card is displayed, read the question and then click the ANSWER box arrow to select an answer. Flip through Flash Cards. If your score is 15 (75%) correct or greater, click Print on the File menu to print your results. If your score is less than 15 (75%) correct, then redo this exercise by clicking the Replay button.

3 Practice Test

Below OneNote Project 2, click the Practice Test link. Answer each question, enter your first and last name at the bottom of the page, and then click the Grade Test button. When the graded practice test is displayed on your screen, click Print on the File menu to print a hard copy. Continue to take practice tests until you score 80% or better.

4 Who Wants To Be a Computer Genius?

Below OneNote Project 2, click the Computer Genius link. Read the instructions, enter your first and last name at the bottom of the page, and then click the PLAY button. When your score is displayed, click the PRINT RESULTS link to print a hard copy.

5 Wheel of Terms

Below OneNote Project 2, click the Wheel of Terms link. Read the instructions, and then enter your first and last name and your school name. Click the PLAY button. When your score is displayed, right-click the score and then click Print on the shortcut menu to print a hard copy.

6 Crossword Puzzle Challenge

Below OneNote Project 2, click the Crossword Puzzle Challenge link. Read the instructions, and then enter your first and last name. Click the SUBMIT button. Work the crossword puzzle. When you are finished, click the Submit button. When the crossword puzzle is redisplayed, click the Print button to print a hard copy.

7 Tips and Tricks

Below OneNote Project 2, click the Tips and Tricks link. Click a topic that pertains to Project 2. Right-click the information and then click Print on the shortcut menu. Construct a brief example of what the information relates to in OneNote to confirm you understand how to use the tip or trick.

8 Newsgroups

Below OneNote Project 2, click the Newsgroups link. Click a topic that pertains to Project 2. Print three comments.

9 Expanding Your Horizons

Below OneNote Project 2, click the Expanding Your Horizons link. Click a topic that pertains to Project 2. Print the information. Construct a brief example of what the information relates to in OneNote to confirm you understand the contents of the article.

10 Search Sleuth

Below OneNote Project 2, click the Search Sleuth link. To search for a term that pertains to this project, select a term below the Project 2 title and then use the Google search engine at google.com (or any major search engine) to display and print two Web pages that present information on the term.

11 OneNote Online Training

Below OneNote Project 2, click the OneNote Online Training link. When your browser displays the Office on Microsoft.com Web page, click the OneNote link. Click one of the OneNote courses that covers one or more of the objectives listed at the beginning of the project on page ONE 66. Print the first page of the course before stepping through it.

12 Office Marketplace

Below OneNote Project 2, click the Office Marketplace link. When your browser displays the Office on Microsoft.com Web page, click the Office Marketplace link. Click a topic that relates to OneNote. Print the first page.

Apply Your Knowledge

1 Organizing Class Notes in OneNote

Instructions: Jenny Sitts has enjoyed using OneNote in her database class. Because she anticipates using OneNote for other classes, she would like to organize her notebook. Start OneNote. Perform the following tasks:

1. Create a new folder within the Assignments folder in your notebook. Name the folder, AYK Assignments.
2. Move the Apply Your Knowledge section to this new folder.
3. Rename the Apply Your Knowledge section as AYK 1.
4. Rename the page Class Notes 1.
5. Insert a new section within the AYK Assignments folder. Name the section, AYK 2.
6. Change the title of the page in this new section from Untitled to Class Notes 2.
7. Add the containers and the text shown in Figure 2-73 to the Class Notes 2 page.

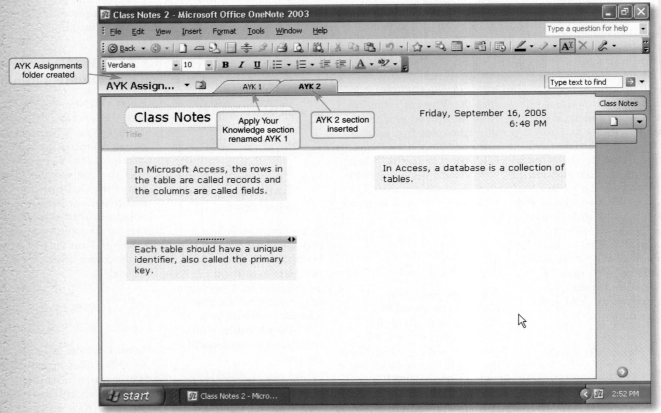

FIGURE 2-73

8. Check spelling.
9. Print the Class Notes 2 page.
10. Search the current folder for the term, record.
11. On the bottom on the printed Class Notes 2 page, write the number of items retrieved by the search.
12. Navigate to the Assignments folder.
13. Quit OneNote.

1 Organizing Tasks in OneNote

Problem: Cordelia Lee has been asked to participate in an undergraduate student research symposium. She has several tasks that she must do to prepare for the symposium.

Instructions: Start OneNote. Perform the following tasks:

1. Create a folder within the Assignments folder. Name the folder, ITL Assignments.
2. Move the In the Lab 1 section to the ITL Assignments folder. Rename the section as ITL 1-1.
3. Add a new section to the folder. Name this section, ITL 2-1.
4. Move to the Scholarship Requirements page in the ITL 1-1 section.
5. Cordelia has completed the scholarship application form. Place a check mark in the check box for that item.
6. Move to the ITL 2-1 section, and rename the Untitled page as Research Symposium.
7. Add a container to this page. Enter the following bulleted list of tasks that Cordelia must accomplish before the symposium.
   Tasks:
   - Write abstract
   - Prepare PowerPoint presentation
   - Complete online registration
   - Rehearse presentation
8. Print the current page.
9. Create a side note for this page that contains the following text:
   Ask Science Club if I can rehearse at the next meeting.
10. Assign the Important note flag to the side note.
11. Print the current page.
12. View the Note Flags task pane, and limit the search to the current folder.
13. Create and print a summary page.
14. Quit OneNote.

In the Lab

2 Organizing Lesson Plans in OneNote

Problem: John Sanchez has found OneNote very useful for organizing his lesson plan ideas. He would like to organize his lesson plans and use some of the stationery templates in OneNote.

Instructions: Open OneNote. Perform the following tasks:

1. If necessary, create a folder named ITL Assignments within the Assignments folder.
2. Move the In the Lab 2 section to the ITL Assignments folder. Rename the section as ITL 1-2.
3. Add a new section to the folder. Name this section, ITL 2-2.
4. Use the Lecture Notes and Study Questions stationery in the Academic category and add the text shown in Figure 2-74 to the Excel Lesson Plan page.

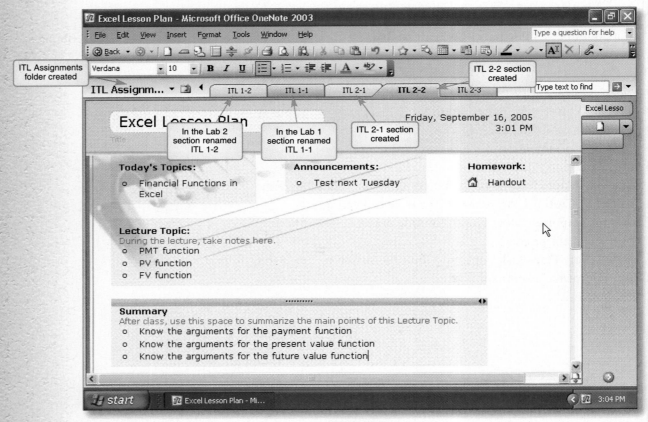

FIGURE 2-74

5. If you have an Untitled page (see Figure 2-74), delete the page.
6. Print the Excel Lesson Plan page.
7. Quit OneNote.

In the Lab

3 Organizing a Family History in OneNote

Problem: Curt Jones maternal grandmother, Grace is celebrating her 65th birthday next year. Curt has decided to surprise his grandmother with a book that contains her family history.

Instructions: Open OneNote and create a folder (if necessary) named ITL Assignments within the Assignments folder.

Instructions Part 1: Move the In the Lab 3 section to the ITL Assignments folder and rename the section as ITL 1-3. Create a new section with the name ITL 2-3.

Instructions Part 2: Copy the Family History page from section ITL 1-3 to section ITL 2-3. If you have an Untitled page in the section after the copy is complete, delete the Untitled page. Remove all the note flags from the list of items. (*Hint*: Use the Note Flags button arrow.)

Instructions Part 3: Modify the outline on the Family History page in section ITL 2-3 to include items below item 4b (From outside sources). These items are:
    i. Published genealogies
    ii. WWW

1. Print the new outline and then collapse the outline to level 2 and print again. Expand the outline.
2. Quit OneNote.

Cases and Places

The difficulty of these case studies varies:
■ are the least difficult and ■■ are the most difficult. The last exercise is a group exercise.

1 ■ You recently performed a price comparison on six food items and entered the data in OneNote. You now realize that you can use this comparison as part of a class assignment but you need to reorganize your notes first. Create a folder within the Assignments folder called C&P Assignments. Move section C&P 1 to this folder and rename section C&P 1 as C&P 1-1. Create a new section called C&P 2-1 that includes a Food List page. Place a bulleted list on this page that shows each store you visited and lists below the store the items that were the least expensive. You should have two levels of bullets. Use an Important note flag next to identify the item that had the greatest price difference.

2 ■ You and your friends have invested a considerable amount of time in preparing for the city wide garage sale/flea market. You realize that you have not done any financial analysis and would like to add this to the notes you already have in OneNote. Before you do, however, you realize that it would be good to reorganize your notebook. If necessary, create a folder within the Assignments folder called C&P Assignments. Move section C&P 2 to this folder and rename section C&P 2 as C&P 1-2. Create a new section named C&P 2-2. Copy the page and subpage from section C&P 1-2 to C&P 2-2. If necessary, group the page and the subpage. Create another subpage that lists anticipated revenues and expenses for the garage sale. Include a side note that reminds you to check on the disposal of unsold items.

3 ■■ You have been very pleased with the sample flyer you created advertising your pet sitting services. Recently, you discovered that OneNote has templates available that you can use. You would like to create a flyer using one of the stationery templates and compare it to the previous version. If necessary, create a folder within the Assignments folder called C&P Assignments. Move section C&P 3 to this folder and rename section C&P 3 as C&P 1-3. Create a new section named C&P 2-3. Use one of the templates in the Decorative stationery category and redesign your brochure. Check your spelling.

4 ■■ Now that you have used OneNote to design a sample Web page for the Career Placement Office, you would like to determine what else you need to do to ensure a successful job search. If necessary, create a folder within the Assignments folder called C&P Assignments. Move section C&P 4 to this folder and rename section C&P 4 as C&P 1-4. Create a new section named C&P 2-4. Prepare an outline (numbered list) that identifies important factors in conducting a job search. Contact your Career Placement Office or search the Web to research these factors. Include at least one side note with an issue that you think is critical for follow-up.

5 ■■ **Working Together** OneNote has many different stationery templates. Have each team member select a different stationery template and create a brief (one-page) resume. Print the resumes and compare the different styles. As a team, decide which stationery would be best for a resume. Document the advantages and disadvantages of each style.

MICROSOFT

Office OneNote 2003

Integrating OneNote with Other Applications

CASE PERSPECTIVE

Alyssa Ashton is comfortable with using OneNote for course-related notes and projects. She knows how to use folders to organize her notes and how to move pages and sections to other notebook locations. Alyssa can navigate through her notebook easily, searching for specific text and locating flagged items. She uses the Side Notes feature to take brief notes and create reminders of future tasks.

Recently, she was asked to serve on the Alumni Weekend Committee. Alyssa has decided to use OneNote to help her with this volunteer assignment. One of the other committee members has written a draft of the announcement letter in Word. Alyssa would like to copy the draft to OneNote so she can make additional notes. She also wants to be able to use the Research feature of OneNote to investigate further any topics that she does not understand completely.

One of Alyssa's assignments is the special event on Saturday morning. Alyssa has received prices from the college's catering service and needs to estimate the total cost. These calculations would be easier in Excel, so she would like to copy these prices into an Excel worksheet. Planning this special event will require several meetings with others on the Alumni Weekend Committee. Alyssa would like to use the audio features of OneNote to record these meetings.

As you read through the Integration Feature, you will learn how to use the OneNote features that can help you perform various integration tasks, such as those described in the Alyssa Ashton volunteer assignment.

Objectives

You will have mastered the material in this Integration Feature when you can:

- Paste content between OneNote and other Office programs
- Use the Research capabilities of OneNote
- Share OneNote files
- Take and use audio notes in OneNote

Introduction

Integrating OneNote with other applications is a simple process. You can copy content from another application, for example Word, and then paste it into a page in OneNote. Figure 1a on the next page shows text that originally was entered in Word. The text was copied and then pasted into the Alumni Letter page. You also can copy content in OneNote and then paste it into other applications.

Also while working in OneNote, you can perform research by using the Research task pane. You can find material on the topic in which you are interested from a variety of sources. Once you have found the information you want, you can paste part or all of it to a page in your notebook (Figure 1b). When you do, OneNote automatically adds a link to the Web page containing the information.

If you have a microphone, you can record audio notes in OneNote. During the recording, you also can type notes into the notebook. The typed notes play two important roles. First, they act as bookmarks into the audio note. In Figure 1c, for example, the note container that begins with Mary's comment contains notes taken during a recording. The pointer currently is pointing in front of the note that reads,

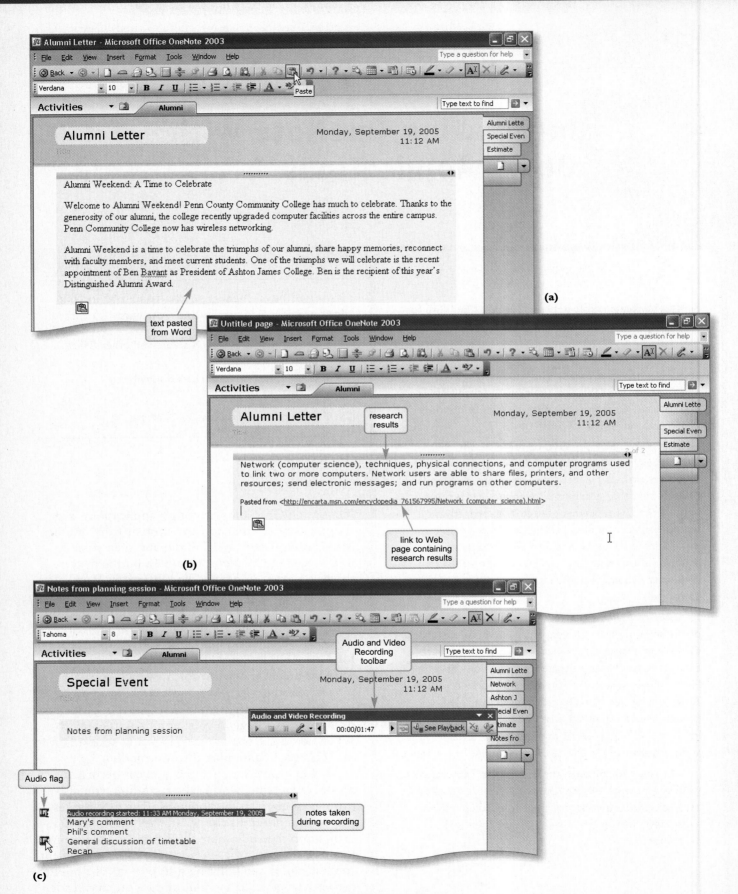

FIGURE 1

General discussion of timetable. When you point to that position, an Audio flag appears. If you click the Audio flag, the playback will begin at the position in the recording at which you began typing this particular note. These notes also play a role when you play back the entire audio note. When the playback arrives at the point at which the typing of a note began, that note will be highlighted. This gives you a visual clue of the progression through the playback of the audio note.

Starting and Customizing OneNote

If you are stepping through this Integration Feature on a computer and you want your screen to match the figures in this book, then you should change your computer's resolution to 800 × 600. For more information on how to change the resolution on your computer, see the Appendix.

The following steps show how to start OneNote.

To Start and Customize OneNote

1 **Click the Start button on the Windows taskbar, point to All Programs on the Start menu, and then point to Microsoft Office on the All Programs submenu.**

2 **Click Microsoft Office OneNote 2003.**

3 **If the Standard and Formatting toolbars are positioned on the same row, click the Toolbar Options button and then click Show Buttons on Two Rows.**

OneNote starts. After several seconds, OneNote displays the notebook. The Standard and Formatting toolbars are on two rows.

> Note: If you are instructed to use a special location for your notebook (for example, on a floppy disk in drive A), you need to perform the following steps as soon as you have started OneNote:
>
> 1. Click Tools on the menu bar and then click Options on the Tools menu.
> 2. Click Open and Save in the Category list in the Options dialog box.
> 3. Click My Notebook in the Paths area and then click the Modify button.
> 4. When OneNote displays the Select Folder dialog box, select the folder where the notebook will be located, click the Select button, and then click the OK button in the Options dialog box. Click the OK button in the Microsoft Office OneNote dialog box.
> 5. Quit OneNote, and then restart OneNote.
>
> For details on the above steps, see the section on Notebook location in the Appendix.

Copying Content Between Applications

You easily can copy content between OneNote and other applications. You select the desired content in the original application, copy the content, transfer to the destination application, and then paste the content. This works whether OneNote is the original application or the destination application.

Before copying content, this section creates the folder, section, and pages that are used in this feature.

Creating a Folder

This section is to be included in a new folder, which requires that a folder be added. The folder is to be positioned just after the Side Notes section. The following steps show how to add a new folder just after the Side Notes section.

To Create a Folder

1

• **If necessary, navigate to the parent folder.**

• **Be sure the Side Notes section is selected.**

• **Click Insert on the menu bar and then click New Folder on the Insert menu.**

2

• **Type** Activities **as the name of the folder and then press the ENTER key.**

The Activities folder now exists in the notebook (Figure 2).

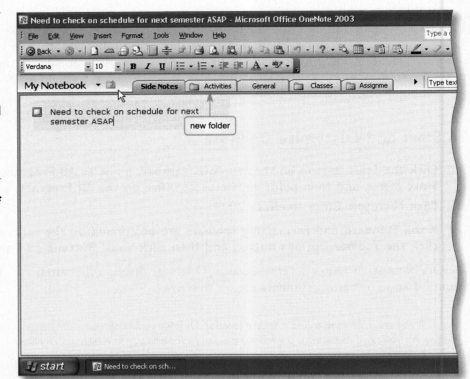

FIGURE 2

The new folder now exists. It currently is empty; that is, it does not contain any sections.

Adding a Section

With the appropriate folder created, you can add a new section. To do so, the folder must be selected. The following steps show how to select the Activities folder and then add the Alumni section to the folder.

To Add a Section

1

• **Click the Activities folder tab.**

The Activities folder is selected (Figure 3). Currently no sections are in the folder.

2

• **Click Insert on the menu bar and then click New Section on the Insert menu to create a section.**

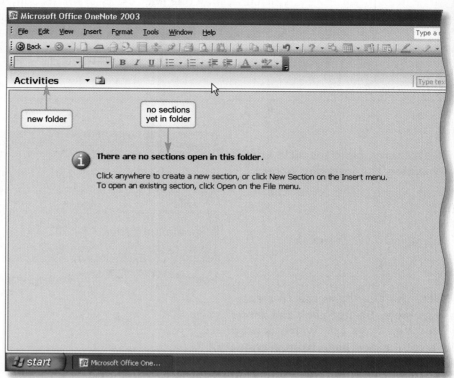

FIGURE 3

3

• **Type** Alumni **as the name of the section.**

The Alumni section exists within the Activities folder (Figure 4).

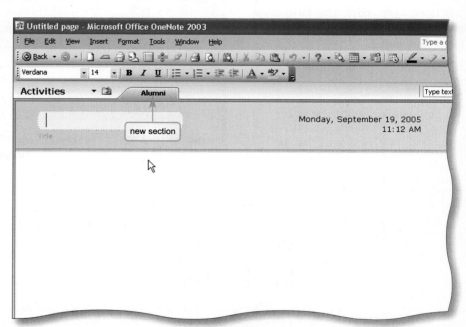

FIGURE 4

Both the Activities folder and the Alumni section currently are selected. Any pages added at this point will be placed in the Alumni section.

Creating Pages

The Alumni section is to contain two pages: Alumni Letter and Special Event. Currently, only one page exists in the section, and it is untitled. The easiest way to create the two pages is to change the title of the untitled page and then create a second page. The following steps show how to change the title of the untitled page to Alumni Letter and then create a section page titled Special Event.

To Create Pages

1

• **If necessary, click the title area to position the insertion point.**

• **Type** Alumni Letter **as the title.**

The page has a title (Figure 5).

FIGURE 5

2

• **Click the New Page tab to create a new page. Do not click the arrow in the New Page tab, which is used to create a new page from stationery.**

3

• **If necessary, click the title area of the new page to position the insertion point.**

• **Type** Special Event **as the title.**

The page now has a title (Figure 6).

FIGURE 6

The Alumni section of the Activities folder now contains two pages, Alumni Letter and Special Event.

Adding a Table

The table to be added to the Special Event page is similar to the table you added on page ONE 45. Recall that you add tables by constructing horizontal outlines. To do so, you use the TAB key, the ENTER key, and the BACKSPACE key as illustrated in the following steps.

To Add a Table

1

- **Click near the upper-left corner of the page area.**
- **Type** `Date` **in the container, and then press the TAB key to produce a second column.**
- **Type** `November 12` **in the second column, and then press the ENTER key to move to the second column in the second row.**

2

- **Press the BACKSPACE key to move back to the first column.**
- **Using the TAB, ENTER, and BACKSPACE keys as in the above steps, enter the remainder of the table shown in Figure 7.**

The table is created.

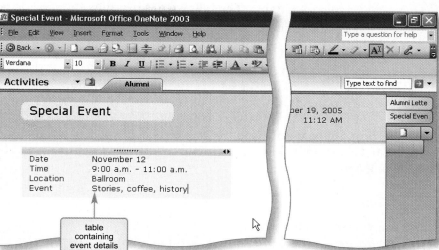

FIGURE 7

Adding a Note

In addition to the table, the Special Event page also contains a note. The following step shows how to add the note to the Special Event page.

To Add a Note

1

- **Click below the table (outside the container), and then enter the note shown in Figure 8.**

The note is entered.

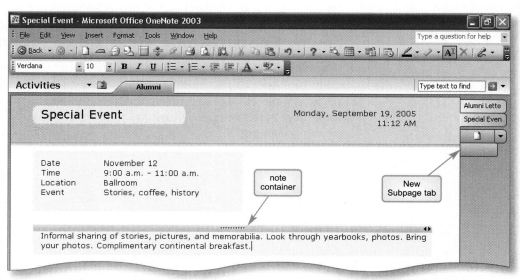

FIGURE 8

Creating a Table on a Subpage

In addition to the table on the Special Event page, the subpage also includes a table. The following steps show how to add a subpage and then create a table on the subpage.

To Create a Table on a Subpage

1

• **Click the New Subpage tab (see Figure 8 on the previous page) to create a subpage.**

2

• **Using the TAB, ENTER, and BACKSPACE keys as illustrated in the previous section (page ONE 119), create the table shown in Figure 9.**

The table is created.

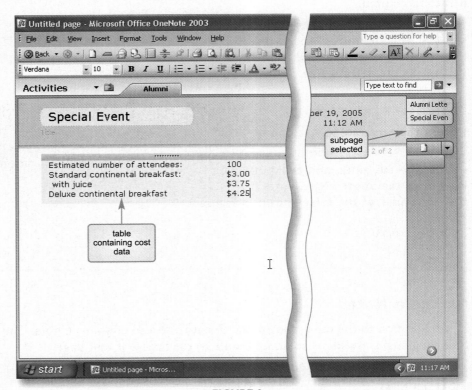

FIGURE 9

Copying Content from Other Office Programs to OneNote

You can copy content from other Office programs to OneNote by copying the data in the other Office application and then pasting it into a page in OneNote. You also have some control as to how the content is pasted. The following steps show how to copy content from Word and then paste the content into OneNote.

To Copy Content from Word to OneNote

1

• **Click the Start button on the Windows taskbar, point to All Programs on the Start menu, point to Microsoft Office on the All Programs submenu, and then click Microsoft Office Word 2003 on the Microsoft Office submenu.**

• **Open the Alumni Weekend document on your Data Disk.**

• **Select the text to be copied by pointing to the beginning of the text to be selected, and then drag right and down to the end of the text to be selected.**

The text to be pasted is selected (Figure 10).

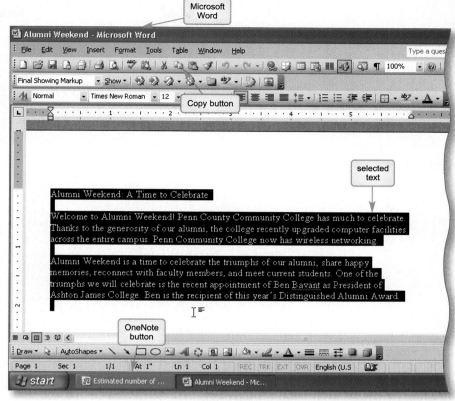

FIGURE 10

2

• **Click the Copy button on the Standard toolbar (see Figure 10).**

• **Click the OneNote button on the Windows taskbar.**

• **Click the Alumni Letter page tab to select the Alumni Letter page.**

• **Make sure the insertion point is in the upper-left corner of the page.**

• **Click the Paste button on the Standard toolbar.**

The selected text is pasted to the Alumni Letter page (Figure 11).

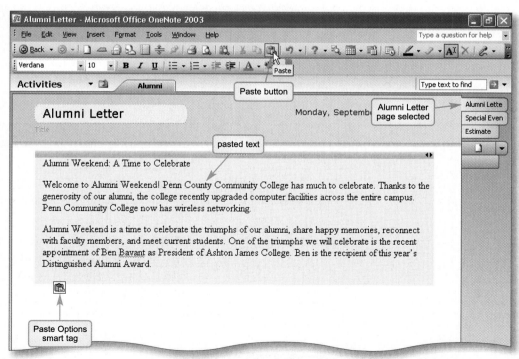

FIGURE 11

When you paste content, OneNote displays the Paste Options smart tag (see Figure 11 on the previous page). A **smart tag** is a button that automatically appears on the screen when OneNote and other Office applications identify certain actions to take based on the type of operation performed. If you click the Paste Options smart tag, OneNote displays a menu of options available for the paste operation (Figure 12). You can use this menu to select how the content is to be pasted.

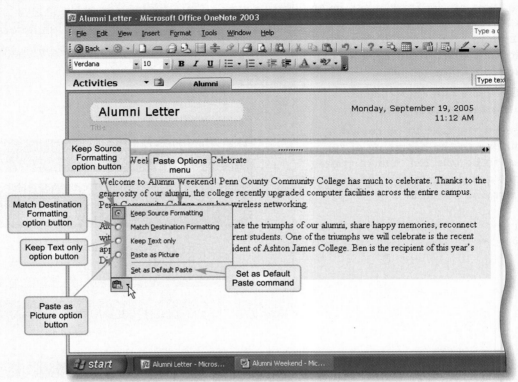

FIGURE 12

Table 1 lists the various options on the Paste Options menu and the effect of the options.

Table 1 Paste Options Smart Tag	
OPTION	EFFECT
Keep Source Formatting	Retains the original formatting as much as possible.
Match Destination Formatting	Matches the format of the note.
Keep Text only	Keeps the text, but removes all formatting.
Paste as Picture	Converts the pasted content to an image. Note that data will not be editable when pasted as a picture.
Set as Default Paste	Sets the selected paste option as the default. This option will be applied in future paste operations.

Quitting Word

Because you are finished using Word, you can quit Word at this point. The following steps show how to quit Word.

To Quit Word

1 Click the Word button on the Windows taskbar.

2 Click the Close button on the Word title bar.

Copying Content from OneNote to Other Office Programs

Just as you can paste content from other Office programs to OneNote, you can paste content from OneNote to other programs. The process is similar. The following steps show how to copy content from OneNote and then paste it into Excel.

To Copy Content from OneNote to Excel

1

• **Click the Start button on the Windows taskbar, point to All Programs on the Start menu, point to Microsoft Office on the All Programs submenu, and then click Microsoft Office Excel 2003 on the Microsoft Office submenu.**

• **If the Getting Started task pane appears, click its Close button.**

• **Click the OneNote button on the Windows taskbar.**

• **Click the Special Event subpage tab.**

• **Click the top edge of the note container on the subpage to select it.**

The Special Event subpage and the note container are selected (Figure 13). Microsoft Excel also is running.

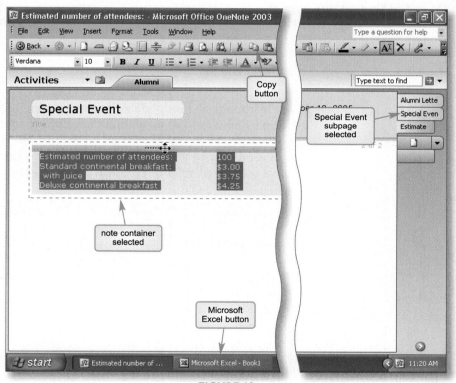

FIGURE 13

2

• **Click the Copy button on the Standard toolbar (see Figure 13 on the previous page).**

• **Click the Excel button on the Windows taskbar.**

• **When the Excel window appears, click the Paste button on the Standard toolbar.**

• **If column A displays # signs, point to the boundary on the right side of the column A heading. When the mouse pointer changes to a split double arrow, drag to the right until the numbers appear.**

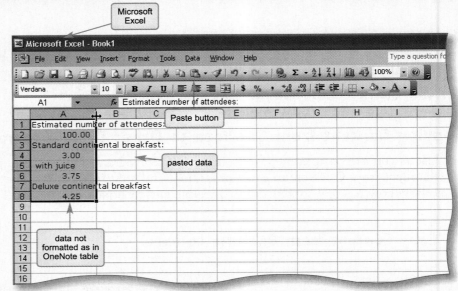

FIGURE 14

The content is pasted to Excel (Figure 14).

Although the individual data items were copied successfully to Excel, the table formatting was lost. Items that should have been in the second column are now on separate rows in the first column. Because the data is all present, however, you still can use Excel to analyze it. You could, for example, create formulas to calculate the total cost given each of the meal items as shown in Figure 15.

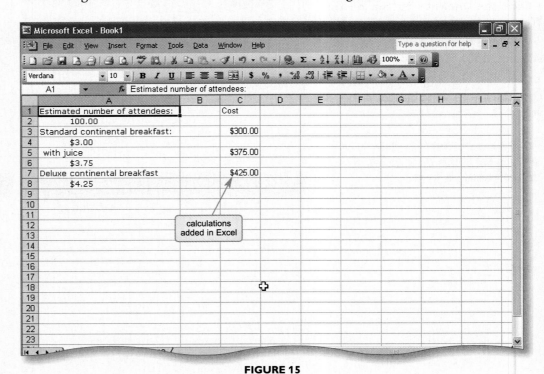

FIGURE 15

The above steps copied a complete note container. You do not need to copy an entire container, however. If you select just a portion of the text within a container before copying and pasting, that portion is all that will be pasted.

Quitting Excel

Because you are finished using Excel, you can quit Excel at this point. The following steps show how to quit Excel.

To Quit Excel

1 Quit Excel by clicking the Close button on the title bar.

2 If Excel displays a dialog box asking if you want to save your changes, click the No button.

Using the Research Task Pane

As you are taking notes, you can use the **Research task pane** to look up information on any topic you choose. In the process, you can access many different research services. Once you have obtained the results you want, you can paste them into your notes. In the process, OneNote automatically will include a link to the Web page that contains the information you pasted. For copying from Web pages, you typically right-click the selected text and then click Copy on the shortcut menu. The following steps show how to perform research and then paste selected text from the research results into your notes.

More About

The Research Task Pane

Other Office applications, such as Excel, Word, and PowerPoint, also use the Research task pane. Internet Explorer uses it too.

To Use the Research Task Pane

1

• **Click the Alumni Letter page tab.**

• **Double-click the word, networking, in the third line of the first paragraph in the note container to select it.**

• **Click Tools on the menu bar and then click Research on the Tools menu.**

• **When OneNote displays the Research task pane, click the reference box arrow (Figure 16).**

The word, networking, is selected in the container, and the Research task pane appears (Figure 16). The selected word appears in the Search for box. The list of available reference sources is displayed.

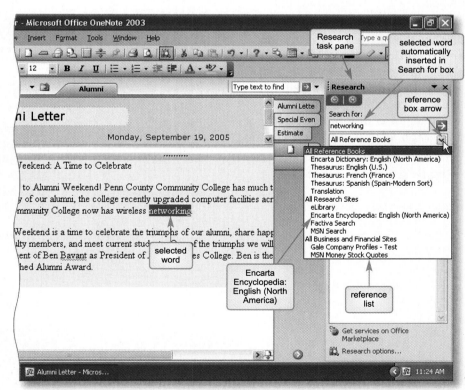

FIGURE 16

2

• **Click Encarta Encyclopedia: English (North America).**

• **After the results appear, point to the I. Introduction link in the Research task pane. (If your list is different, point to any link in your list.)**

The results appear (Figure 17). Because the mouse pointer is positioned over a link, the pointer shape changes to a hand.

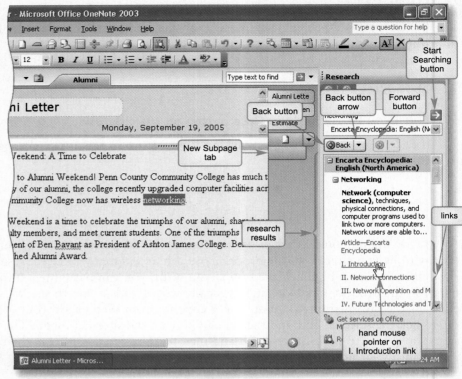

FIGURE 17

3

• **Click the I. Introduction link.**

• **If necessary, scroll down to display the related information, and then drag through the paragraph that begins with the words, Network (computer science), to select it. (If your information is different, select any paragraph within the information that is displayed.)**

• **Right-click the selected text.**

The shortcut menu appears (Figure 18).

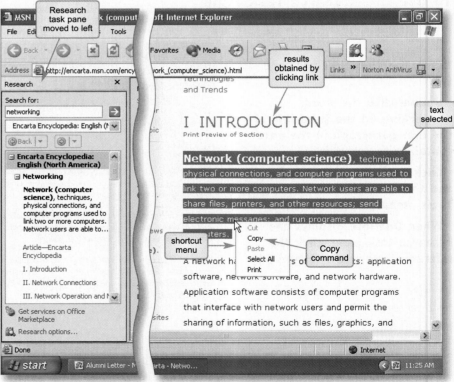

FIGURE 18

4

• **Click Copy on the shortcut menu.**

• **Click the OneNote button on the Windows taskbar.**

• **With the Alumni Letter page selected, click the New Subpage tab (see Figure 17).**

• **If necessary, click near the upper-left corner of the subpage, and then click the Paste button on the Standard toolbar.**

• **Close the Research task pane by clicking its Close button.**

The selected text is pasted to the subpage (Figure 19). OneNote automatically adds a link to the page containing the information at the bottom of the note container.

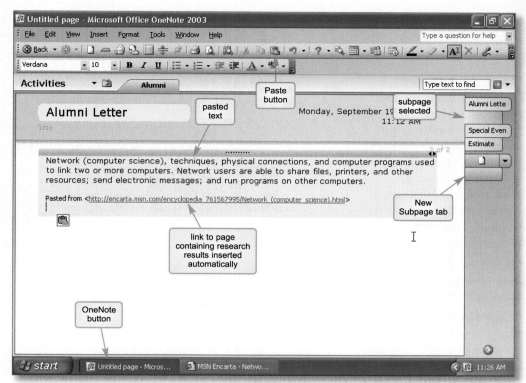

FIGURE 19

After your search results are returned, if you decide to search in a different reference source, click the reference box arrow in the Research task pane and then select the new reference. To view previous items for which you have searched, you can use the Back or Forward buttons in the Research task pane (see Figure 17). You also can click the Back or Forward button arrow to see previous items, and then select an item from the list. To refresh the query, that is, to update the results that are displayed, click the Start Searching button (see Figure 17).

Pasting a Web Page to OneNote

To paste a portion of any Web page to OneNote, you can use the techniques illustrated in Steps 3 and 4 in the previous sequence of steps. If you want to paste a complete Web page, it often is easier to select the entire page by using the Select All command on the Edit menu, as illustrated in the steps on the next page.

Other Ways

1. On Tools menu click Research

More About

The Task Pane

The task pane displays important information and helps you carry out a variety of tasks. There are several different task panes: Help, Search Results, Research, New, and so on. In most cases, the appropriate task pane will appear when needed. If you want to use a task pane and one has not appeared automatically, click View on the menu bar and then click Task Pane on the View menu to display a task pane. If you want a different task pane from the one that currently appears, click the down arrow in the title bar for the task pane and then select the desired task pane in the list that appears.

To Paste a Web Page to OneNote

1

• **Click the Internet Explorer button on the Windows taskbar. (If Internet Explorer is not running, click the Start button on the Windows taskbar, point to All Programs on the Start menu, and then click Internet Explorer on the All Programs submenu.)**

• **If the Research task pane is open, close it by clicking its Close button.**

• **Click the Address box, type** scsite.com/ ac2003/ajc.html **as the address, and then press the ENTER key.**

The Ashton James College home page appears in Internet Explorer (Figure 20).

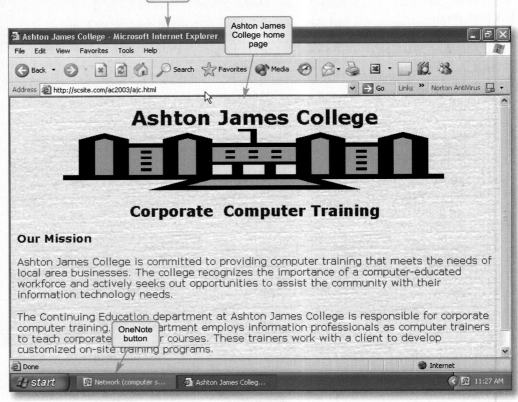

FIGURE 20

2

• **Click Edit on the menu bar and then click Select All on the Edit menu to select the entire page.**

• **Click Edit on the menu bar and then click Copy on the Edit menu.**

• **Click the OneNote button on the Windows taskbar.**

• **Click the New Subpage tab (see Figure 19 on page ONE 127).**

• **Click the Paste button on the Standard toolbar.**

The selected text is pasted to the subpage (Figure 21). OneNote automatically adds a link to the page containing the information at the bottom of the note container.

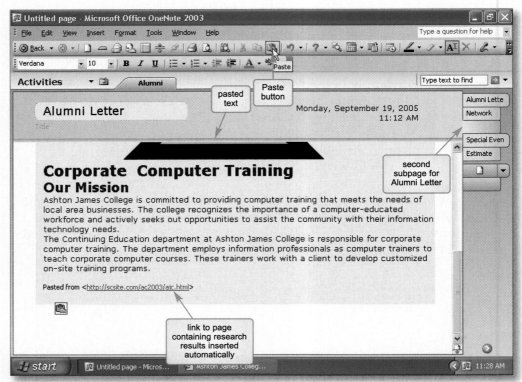

FIGURE 21

3

• **Close the Internet Explorer window by clicking its Close button.**

The format of the pasted version of the Web page is changed slightly, but it contains all the same data. As you scroll the window, you will notice the differences.

Sharing Notes

In OneNote, you can share your notes with others in two ways. You can save any sections you want to share in locations that are accessible to others. You also can e-mail the notes you wish to share.

Saving Sections to Other Locations

By using the Save As command on the File menu, you can save sections to locations other than within the My Notebook folder. Such a section is called a **remote section**. When you create a remote section, OneNote creates a link to the section within the My Notebook folder. You can work with a remote section just as you work with any other section. OneNote signifies the section is a remote section by adding a link icon to the section tab (Figure 22).

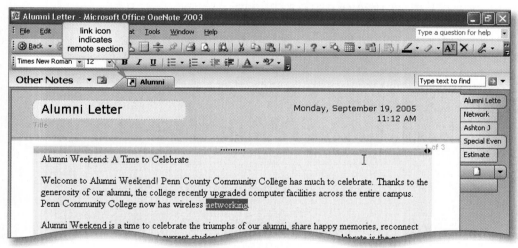

FIGURE 22

Sharing OneNote Files

By saving a section in a shared folder, other users also can have access to the section. Each user would need to open the section from the shared folder, provided, of course, that each one has the ability to do so. The section tab then would have the link icon shown in Figure 22. Although multiple users would have access to the folder, only one user at a time could update the section.

Using OneNote with Outlook

You can send your notes via e-mail with Microsoft Outlook 2003. The next page describes the actions you can perform with Outlook.

TO CREATE AN OUTLOOK TASK

1. Click Tools on the menu bar, point to Create Outlook Item on the Tools menu, and then click Create Outlook Task on the Create Outlook Item submenu.
2. Paste selected text from your notes into the task description window.
3. Save the task.

TO SEND E-MAIL

1. Select the page to e-mail.
2. Click File on the menu bar, point to Send To on the File menu, and then click Mail Recipient on the Send To submenu.
3. Enter the relevant information concerning the recipient and subject.
4. Send the e-mail.

Recording and Playing Notes

In OneNote, you can take audio or video notes. For example, you can record a lecture or a meeting and then later play back the recorded notes. In addition to simply recording the audio notes, however, you also can add typed notes. For instance, you could type the name of a person making a comment or a brief description of the point being made in the lecture. These typed notes serve as bookmarks into the audio notes. When you want to play back the recorded notes, you can use a typed note to start the playback at the precise point where you added the typed note. In addition, if you play back the complete recording, OneNote will highlight each typed comment at the point it occurred in the original audio recording.

To record audio or video notes, you use the **Audio and Video Recording toolbar**. Figure 23 shows the toolbar as well as an audio recording with typed notes. The functions of the various buttons on the toolbar are described in the figure.

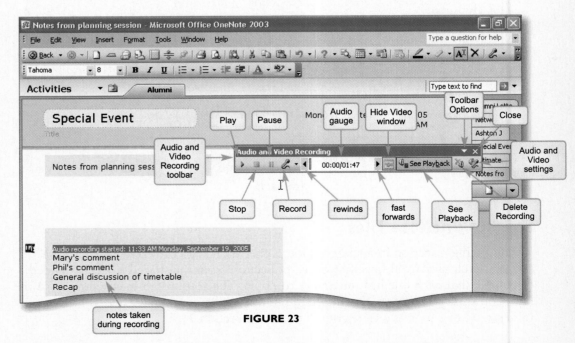

FIGURE 23

To play back notes, you can use the Start button on the Audio and Video Recording toolbar. Usually, however, you will use **Audio flags** in your notes. Figure 24 shows an Audio flag at the beginning of the note container. Clicking this Audio flag causes the playback to begin, starting at the beginning of the recording. If you point in front of a line in the notes, an Audio flag for that line will appear. Clicking that Audio flag also causes the recording to begin, but in this case it will begin at the point in the recording at which you typed that line. In Figure 25, for example, the playback will begin at the precise point you began typing General discussion of timetable.

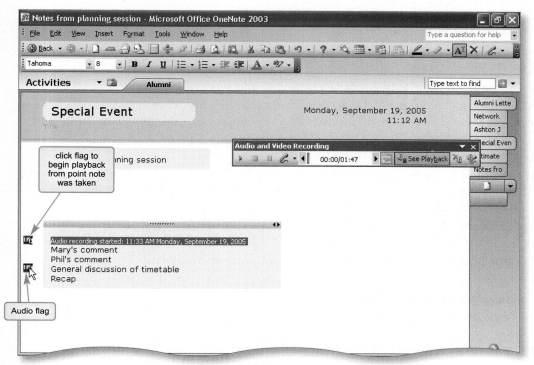

FIGURE 24

When you play back notes and the playback arrives at the point where you added a typed note, the note will be highlighted as shown in Figure 25. In this figure, the recording gauge shows how far the playback has proceeded. The highlight also indicates that the playback has progressed to the point where Phil's comment was typed, but has not yet progressed to the point where General discussion of timetable was typed.

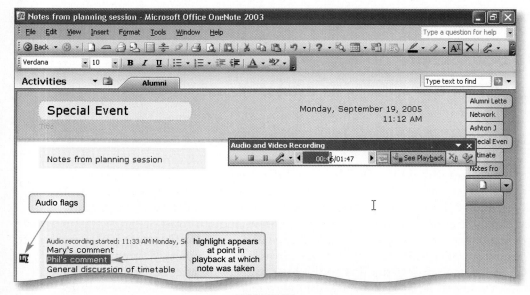

FIGURE 25

More About

The Quick Reference

For a table that lists how to complete the tasks covered in this book using the mouse, menu, shortcut menu, and keyboard, see the Quick Reference Summary at the back of this book or visit the OneNote 2003 Quick Reference Web page (scsite.com/one2003/qr).

Audio notes are stored in separate files on your disk. OneNote assigns names to these files automatically. The name consists of the name of the page followed by a number. If you no longer need an audio note, you can remove it by deleting its note container. OneNote will delete the container from your notebook and also remove the corresponding audio file from your disk.

The following steps show how to perform the various operations associated with recording and playing audio notes.

TO RECORD NOTES

1. Be sure you have a microphone connected and working properly.
2. Unless the Audio and Video Recording toolbar already is on the screen, click View on the menu bar, point to Toolbars on the View menu, and then click Audio and Video Recording.
3. Click the Record button (see Figure 23 on page ONE 130).
4. If you wish, enter notes into the note container for the audio recording during the recording process. Be sure to press the ENTER key after each note so that each individual note is on a separate line in the note container.
5. When the recording is finished click the Stop button (see Figure 23).

TO PLAY BACK RECORDED NOTES FROM A SPECIFIC POSITION

1. Point in front of the line in the note that was taken at the point you want to start the playback to display the Audio flag for that line.
2. Click the Audio flag for the line.

TO PLAY BACK THE ENTIRE RECORDING

1. Point in front of the beginning of the note container for the recording to display the Audio flag.
2. Click the Audio flag.

Quitting OneNote

The Integration Feature is complete and you are ready to quit OneNote. The following step shows how to quit OneNote.

To Quit OneNote

1 **Click the Close button on the OneNote title bar.**

Integration Feature Summary

The Integration Feature illustrated the ways in which OneNote can be integrated with other applications. You first created the folder, section, and pages used in this feature. You then learned how to copy content from another application to OneNote and also how to copy from OneNote to other applications. This feature then introduced you to the research capabilities of OneNote to find information about a topic of interest from a variety of sources. You learned how to paste the results to a OneNote page and saw how OneNote includes a link to the page containing the information automatically. You learned how to paste a complete Web page to a OneNote page and saw that OneNote again inserted a link to the Web page automatically. You learned about different ways of sharing notes with others. Finally, you learned how to record and play back audio notes. The feature illustrated how you can take a collection of typed notes along with the audio notes and then easily begin the playback at the point where you began typing a note. Also, during playback, whenever OneNote arrived at a point where you typed a note, OneNote would highlight the note.

What You Should Know

Having completed this Integration Feature, you now should be able to perform the tasks below. The tasks are listed in the same order they were presented in this feature. For a list of the buttons, menus, toolbars, and commands introduced in this feature, see the Quick Reference Summary at the back of this book, and refer to the Page Number column.

1. Start and Customize OneNote (ONE 115)
2. Create a Folder (ONE 116)
3. Add a Section (ONE 117)
4. Create Pages (ONE 118)
5. Add a Table (ONE 119)
6. Add a Note (ONE 119)
7. Create a Table on a Subpage (ONE 120)
8. Copy Content from Word to OneNote (ONE 121)
9. Quit Word (ONE 123)
10. Copy Content from OneNote to Excel (ONE 123)
11. Quit Excel (ONE 125)
12. Use the Research Task Pane (ONE 125)
13. Paste a Web Page to OneNote (ONE 128)
14. Create an Outlook Task (ONE 130)
15. Send E-Mail (ONE 130)
16. Record Notes (ONE 132)
17. Play Back Recorded Notes from a Specific Position (ONE 132)
18. Play Back the Entire Recording (ONE 132)
19. Quit OneNote (ONE 132)

1 Integrating OneNote with Excel and Internet Explorer

Problem: The university has agreed to cover Cordelia Lee's expenses for her participation in an undergraduate student research symposium. She must copy her anticipated expenses to Excel. Because the symposium will be held at a different school, she also would like to learn something about the school.

Instructions: Start OneNote. Perform the following tasks:

1. Open the Assignments folder and then open the ITL Assignments folder.
2. Add a new section to the folder. Name this section, ITL IF-1.
3. Rename the untitled page as Symposium Expenses.
4. Enter the text shown in Figure 26 to the page.

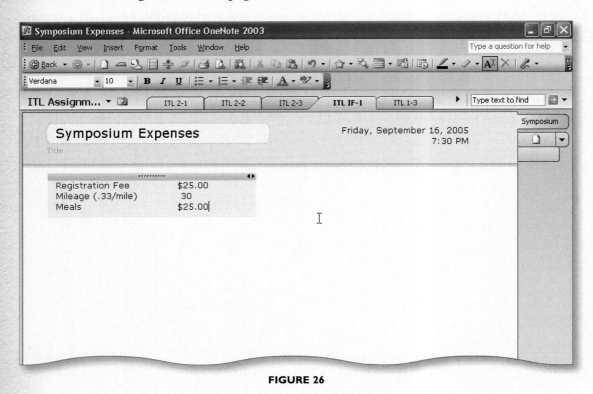

FIGURE 26

5. Start Excel and copy the text on the Symposium Expenses page to Excel.
6. Adjust the width of column A so that the numbers appear. Print the worksheet.
7. Create a new subpage for the Symposium Expenses page.
8. Copy the Ashton James College Web page (scsite.com/ac2003/ajc.html) to this subpage.
9. Print the current page.
10. Quit Excel, Internet Explorer, and OneNote.

In the Lab

2 Integrating OneNote with Word and Performing Research

Problem: John Sanchez is on the Faculty Search Committee. The committee is hiring a full-time faculty member to teach bioinformatics. Another member of the committee has prepared an initial draft of the advertisement in Word. John would like to copy this draft to OneNote for further revision. He also would like to learn more about bioinformatics.

Instructions: Start OneNote. Perform the following tasks:

1. Open the Assignments folder and then open the ITL Assignments folder.
2. Add a new section to the folder. Name this section, ITL IF-2.
3. Rename the untitled page as CS Search Committee.
4. Open the CS Advertisement document in Word. The document is on your Data Disk.
5. Copy the document to OneNote and print the current page.
6. Highlight the word bioinformatics and search Encarta Encyclopedia (English) for the term. Click the link in your list. When the results appear, find the paragraph shown in Figure 27 and copy it to a new subpage in OneNote. (If your list is different, point to any link in the list and copy a paragraph that contains the word, bioinformatics.)

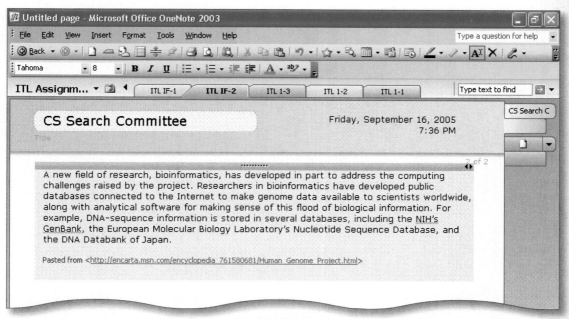

FIGURE 27

7. Print the current page.
8. Quit Word, Internet Explorer, and OneNote.

Appendix A

Changing Screen Resolution and Customizing OneNote

This appendix explains how to change your screen resolution in Windows to the resolution used in this book. It also describes how to reset the OneNote toolbars and menus to their installation settings and how to customize OneNote.

Changing Screen Resolution

The **screen resolution** indicates the number of pixels (dots) that your system uses to display the letters, numbers, graphics, and background you see on your screen. The screen resolution usually is stated as the product of two numbers, such as 800×600. An 800×600 screen resolution results in a display of 800 distinct pixels on each of 600 lines, or about 480,000 pixels. The figures in this book were created using a screen resolution of 800×600.

The screen resolutions most commonly used today are 800×600 and 1024×768, although some Office specialists operate their computers at a much higher screen resolution, such as 2048×1536. The following steps show how to change the screen resolution from 1024×768 to 800×600.

To Change the Screen Resolution

1

- **If necessary, minimize all applications so that the Windows desktop appears.**
- **Right-click the Windows desktop.**

Windows displays the Windows desktop shortcut menu (Figure A-1).

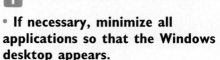

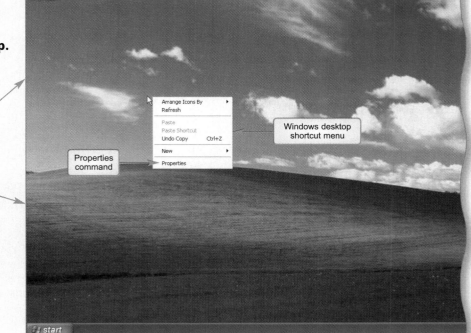

FIGURE A-1

2

• **Click Properties on the shortcut menu.**

• **When Windows displays the Display Properties dialog box, click the Settings tab.**

Windows displays the Settings sheet in the Display Properties dialog box (Figure A-2). The Settings sheet shows a preview of the Windows desktop using the current screen resolution (1024 × 768). The Settings sheet also shows the screen resolution and the Color quality settings.

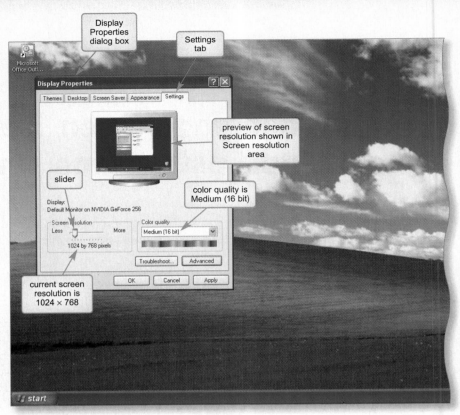

FIGURE A-2

3

• **Drag the slider in the Screen resolution area to the left so that the screen resolution changes to 800 × 600.**

The screen resolution in the Screen resolution area changes to 800 × 600 (Figure A-3). The Settings sheet shows a preview of the Windows desktop using the new screen resolution (800 × 600).

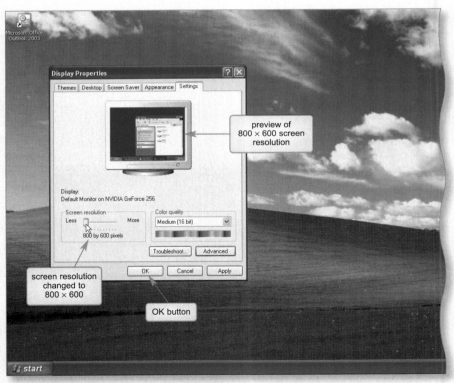

FIGURE A-3

4

• **Click the OK button.**

• **If Windows displays the Monitor Settings dialog box, click the Yes button.**

Windows changes the screen resolution from 1024 × 768 to 800 × 600 (Figure A-4).

800 × 600
screen resolution

FIGURE A-4

As shown in the previous steps, as you decrease the screen resolution, Windows displays less information on your screen, but the information increases in size. The reverse also is true: as you increase the screen resolution, Windows displays more information on your screen, but the information decreases in size.

Resetting the OneNote Toolbars and Menus

In OneNote, you can personalize toolbars and menus. You can change the toolbar or toolbars that appear by using the Toolbars command on the View menu, and then selecting the toolbars you want to appear. You also can change the buttons that appear on a particular toolbar by using the Toolbar Options button (see Figure A-5 on the next page). In addition, OneNote personalizes the commands on the menus based on their usage. Each time you start OneNote, the toolbars and menus have the same settings as the last time you used the application. This appendix shows you how to reset usage data, that is, how to clear menu and toolbar settings. Resetting usage data does not affect the location of the toolbars, nor does it change any buttons you might have added using the Customize dialog box. To reverse these changes, you need to reset the toolbar. The steps on the next page show how to reset the usage data and also the Standard toolbar.

To Reset Menu and Toolbar Usage Data

1

• **Start OneNote.**

• **Click View on the menu bar, and then point to Toolbars on the View menu.**

The View menu appears (Figure A-5). The Toolbars submenu also appears.

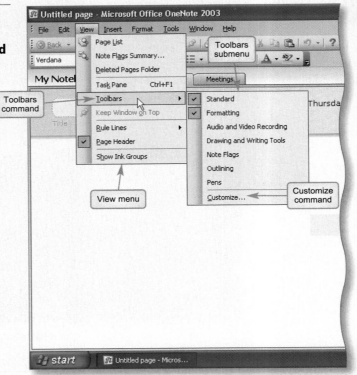

FIGURE A-5

2

• **Click Customize on the Toolbars submenu.**

• **When OneNote displays the Customize dialog box, click the Options tab, if necessary.**

OneNote displays the Customize dialog box (Figure A-6). The Customize dialog box contains three sheets used for customizing the OneNote toolbars and menus.

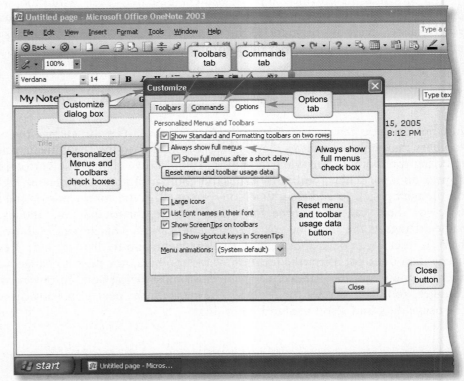

FIGURE A-6

3

• **Click the Reset menu and toolbar usage data button.**

The Microsoft Office OneNote dialog box displays a message indicating the actions that will be taken and asks if you are sure you wish to proceed (Figure A-7).

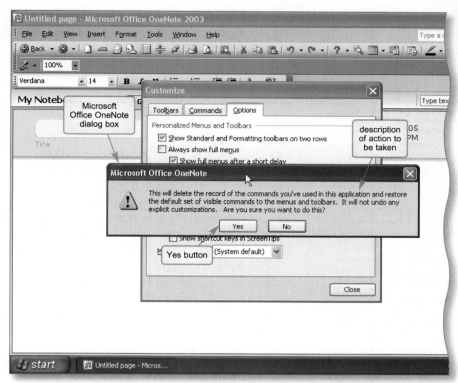

FIGURE A-7

4

• **Click the Yes button in the Microsoft OneNote dialog box.**

• **Click the Toolbars tab in the Customize dialog box, and then click Standard (click the word, Standard, not the check box in front of it) to ensure it is selected in the Toolbars list.**

The Customize dialog box appears (Figure A-8). Standard is selected in the Toolbars list.

5

• **Click the Reset button.**

• **When the Microsoft Office OneNote dialog box appears, asking if you are sure you want to reset the changes made to the Standard toolbar, click the OK button. Repeat the process for any other toolbar you want to reset.**

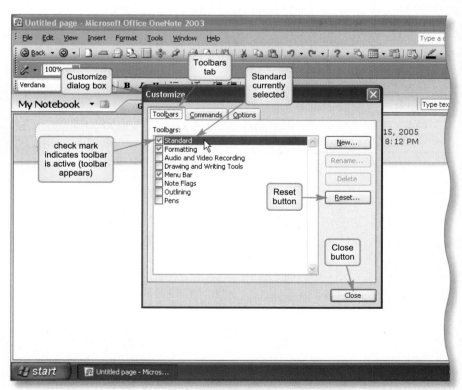

FIGURE A-8

6

• **Click the Close button in the Customize dialog box.**

OneNote resets the Standard toolbar to its installation settings.

Other Ways

1. Click Toolbar Options button, click Add or Remove Buttons button, click Customize, click Options tab, click Reset menu and toolbar usage data button to reset usage data, click Yes button, click Close button
2. Click Toolbar Options button, click Add or Remove Buttons button, click Customize, click Toolbars tab, click toolbar name, click Reset button to reset toolbar to installation settings, click OK button, click Close button
3. Right-click toolbar, click Customize on shortcut menu, click Options tab, click Reset menu and toolbar usage data button to reset usage data, click Yes button, click Close button
4. Right-click toolbar, click Customize on shortcut menu, click Toolbars tab, click toolbar name, click Reset button to reset toolbar to installation settings, click OK button, click Close button

You can turn off short menus by placing a check mark in the Always show full menus check box in the Customize dialog box (see Figure A-6 on page APP 4).

One other task you can complete through the Customize dialog box in Figure A-6 is to add buttons to toolbars and commands to menus. To add buttons, click the Commands tab in the Customize dialog box and then drag the commands to a toolbar. To add commands to a menu, click the Commands tab in the Customize dialog box and then drag the commands to the menu name. When the menu appears, you then can drag the commands to the desired menu location.

OneNote considers the menu bar at the top of the OneNote window to be a toolbar. If you add commands to menus as described in the previous paragraph and want to reset them to their installation settings, do the following: (1) Click View on the menu bar and then point to Toolbars on the View menu; (2) click Customize on the Toolbars submenu; (3) click the Toolbars tab; (4) scroll down in the Toolbars list and click Menu Bar; (5) click the Reset button; (6) click the OK button; and (7) click the Close button.

Hiding Page Titles

Normally, page titles appear on the page tabs (Figure A-9). You can hide these page titles as shown in the following step.

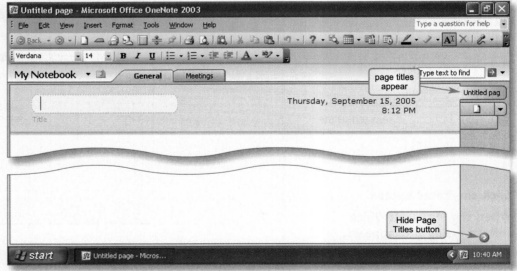

FIGURE A-9

TO HIDE PAGE TITLES

1. Click the Hide Page Titles button (see Figure A-9).

    The page titles no longer appear (Figure A-10). The Hide Page Titles button has become the Show Page Titles button.

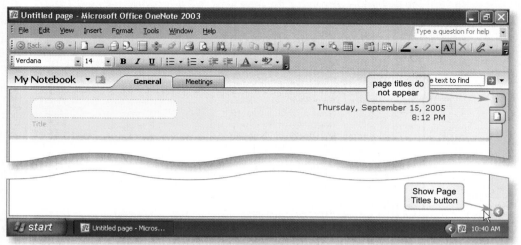

FIGURE A-10

The following step illustrates how to return the titles to the screen using the Show Page Titles button.

TO SHOW PAGE TITLES

1. Click the Show Page Titles button (see Figure A-10).

Changing the Notebook Location

You can customize OneNote in a variety of ways. For the most part, you probably will not need to make any changes to the default choices. One area that you might want to change, however, is the location of the My Notebook folder. The following steps show how to change the location of My Notebook by changing the location of the My Notebook folder to a folder called My Notebook on a disk in drive A. You can use the same steps to change it to any folder on any drive. The folder does not need to be named My Notebook; any folder will work.

To Change the Notebook Location

1

- **Click Tools on the menu bar.**

The Tools menu appears (Figure A-11).

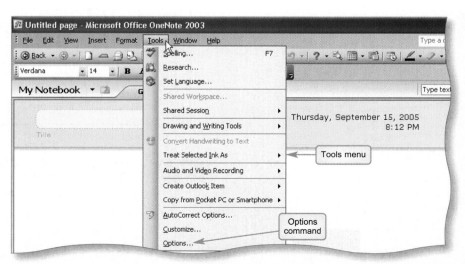

FIGURE A-11

**Microsoft Office
OneNote 2003**

2

- **Click Options on the Tools menu.**
- **Click Open and Save in the Category area.**

The Options dialog box appears (Figure A-12). The Open and Save category is selected.

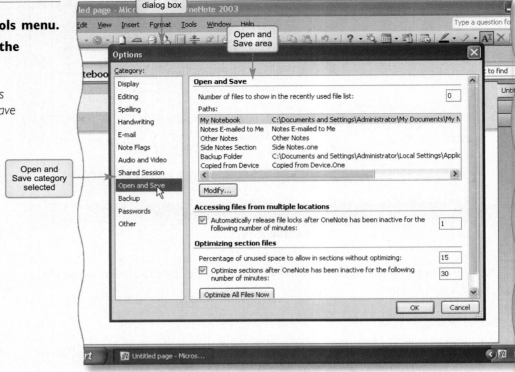

FIGURE A-12

3

- **Click My Notebook in the Paths list.**

My Notebook is selected (Figure A-13).

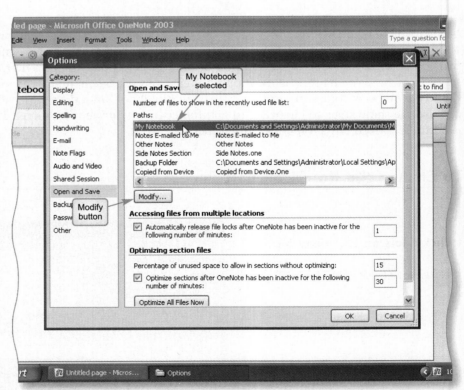

FIGURE A-13

4

- Click the **Modify** button.
- When OneNote displays the Select Folder dialog box, click the **Look in** box arrow, and then click **3½ Floppy (A:)**.
- Click the **My Notebook** folder.

The Select Folder dialog box appears (Figure A-14). Both 3½ Floppy (A:) and the My Notebook folder are selected.

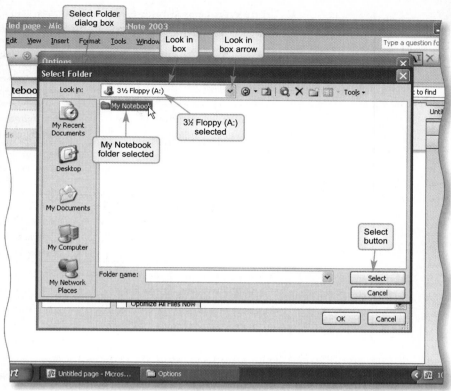

FIGURE A-14

5

- Click the **Select** button in the Select Folder dialog box.

The Options dialog box appears (Figure A-15). The path for My Notebook is changed.

6

- Click the **OK** button in the Options dialog box.
- Click the **OK** button in the Microsoft Office OneNote dialog box.
- If requested to change the location of Notes E-mailed to Me, use the same steps you used to change the location for the notebook.

The location of My Notebook is now changed to the My Notebook folder on the disk in drive A.

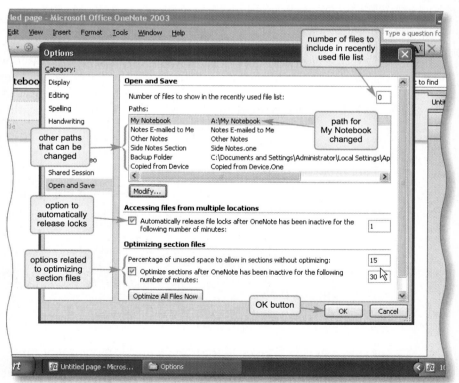

FIGURE A-15

The change will take effect as soon as you quit and then restart OneNote. Other Open and Save options are available. These options are described in Table A-1.

Table A-1 Open and Save Options	
OPTION	DESCRIPTION
Number of files to show in the recently used file list	Enter number of files to be included in the list of recently used files.
Paths	Just as with the path for My Notebook, other paths can be changed for Notes E-mailed to Me, Side Notes Section, and Backup Folder.
Automatically release file locks after OneNote has been inactive for the following number of minutes	If checked and people are sharing OneNote files from multiple locations, file locks will be released automatically after the indicated number of minutes. Otherwise, they will not.
Percentage of unused space to allow in sections without optimizing	Indicates percentage of unused space in a section that will be allowed before OneNote optimizes the section.
Optimize sections after OneNote has been inactive for the following number of minutes	If checked, sections will be optimized automatically after OneNote has been active for the indicated number of minutes.
Optimize All Files Now	Click the button to immediately optimize all files in the notebook.

Additional Customizations

A variety of other customizations are possible when you click Tools on the menu bar and then click Options on the Tools menu. They are described in the following sections. Unless you have some very special need, you should retain the default settings, leaving them the way they are normally set, that is, the way they are shown in the following figures.

Display

The Display options are shown in Figure A-16. The options are described in Table A-2.

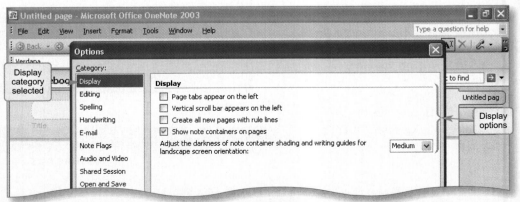

FIGURE A-16

Table A-2 Display Options

OPTION	DESCRIPTION
Page tabs appear on the left	If checked, page tabs will be on left. Otherwise, they will be on right.
Vertical scroll bar appears on the left	If checked, vertical scroll bar will be on left. Otherwise, it will be on right.
Create all new pages with rule lines	If checked, all pages will begin with rule lines. Otherwise, they will not.
Show note containers on pages	If checked, container boxes will appear. Otherwise, they will not.
Adjust the darkness of note container shading and writing guides for landscape screen orientation	Select desired darkness. Default is Medium.

Editing

The Editing options are shown in Figure A-17. The options are described in Table A-3 on the next page. Your option list may be different.

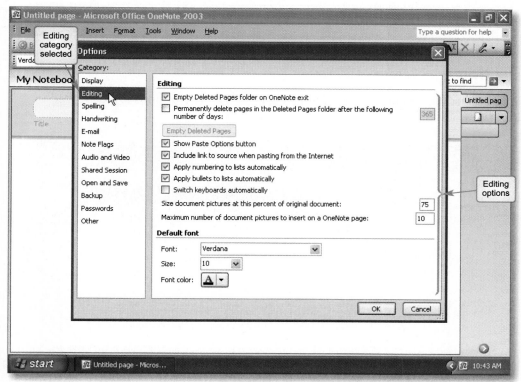

FIGURE A-17

Table A-3   Editing Options

OPTION	DESCRIPTION
Empty Deleted Pages folder on OneNote exit	If checked, Deleted Pages folder will be emptied automatically whenever you exit OneNote.
Permanently delete pages in the Deleted Pages folder after the following number of days	Select desired number of days to dictate how often pages will be deleted permanently.
Show Paste Options button	If checked, the Paste Options button appears during certain paste operations. Otherwise, it does not.
Include link to source when pasting from the Internet	If checked, the link to source will appear when pasting from the Internet. Otherwise, it will not.
Apply numbering to lists automatically	If checked, numbering in lists is automatic. Otherwise, it is not.
Apply bullets to lists automatically	If checked, bulleting in lists is automatic. Otherwise, it is not.
Switch keyboards automatically	If checked, will switch between keyboards automatically. Otherwise, it will not.
Font	Change default font.
Size	Change default font size.
Font color	Change default font color.

Spelling

The Spelling options are shown in Figure A-18. The options are described in Table A-4.

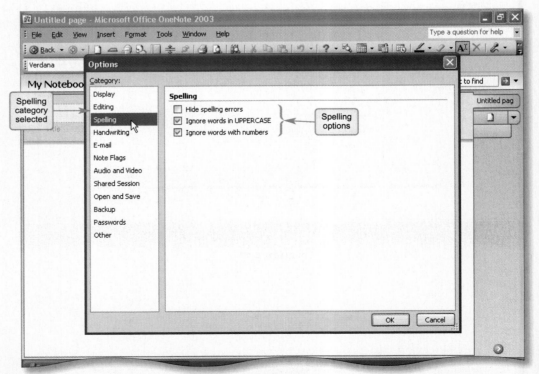

FIGURE A-18

Table A-4 Spelling Options

OPTION	DESCRIPTION
Hide spelling errors	If checked, spelling errors will be hidden. If not, they will appear.
Ignore words in UPPERCASE	If checked, words in uppercase will be ignored during spell check. Otherwise, they will be included.
Ignore words with numbers	If checked, words containing numbers will be ignored during spell check. Otherwise, they will be included.

Handwriting

The Handwriting options are shown in Figure A-19. The options are described in Table A-5.

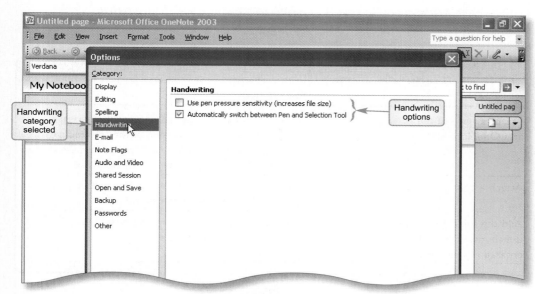

FIGURE A-19

Table A-5 Handwriting Options

OPTION	DESCRIPTION
Use pen pressure sensitivity (increases file size)	If checked, pen pressure sensitivity will be used during pen operations. (Pressing harder with the pen results in thicker ink strokes.) If not, it will not. Note that the device you are using to write or draw must support pen pressure sensitivity in order for this to be effective.
Automatically switch between Pen and Selection Tool	If checked and you switch from using a pen to using a mouse, will automatically switch to Selection Tool. Otherwise, it will not and remains in Pen mode.

E-Mail

The E-mail options are shown in Figure A-20. The options are described in Table A-6 on the next page.

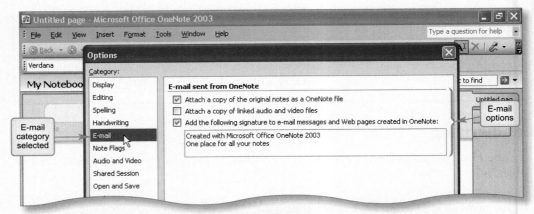

FIGURE A-20

Table A-6 E-mail Options	
OPTION	DESCRIPTION
Attach a copy of the original notes as a OneNote file	If checked, in addition to the body of the message, which contains an HTML version of the selected pages, the notes to be sent also will be attached as a OneNote (.ONE) file. If not, only the HTML version is sent.
Attach a copy of linked audio files	If checked, a copy of linked audio files will be attached automatically. Otherwise, it will not.
Add the following signature to e-mail messages and Web pages created in OneNote	If checked, indicated signature will be added. automatically. Otherwise, it will not.

Note Flags

The Note Flags options are shown in Figure A-21. The options are described in Table A-7.

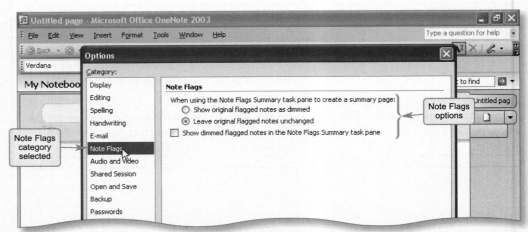

FIGURE A-21

Table A-7 Note Flags Options

OPTION	DESCRIPTION
When using Note Flags Summary task pane to create a summary page	Choose between two actions to be taken: Show original flagged notes as dimmed or Leave original notes flags unchanged.
Show dimmed flagged notes in the Note Flags Summary task pane	If checked, dimmed flag notes will appear in the Note Flags Summary task pane. Otherwise, they will not.

Audio and Video

The Audio and Video options are shown in Figure A-22. The options are described in Table A-8.

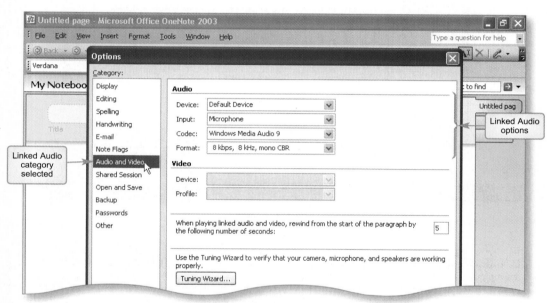

FIGURE A-22

Table A-8 Audio and Video Options

OPTION	DESCRIPTION
Device	Indicate sound recording hardware.
Input	Select input for audio.
Codec	Indicate codec, that is, a program that instructs the computer how to play a media clip.
Format	Indicate audio format.
Device	Indicate video recording hardware.
Profile	Indicate profile for video hardware.
When playing linked audio and video, rewind from start of the paragraph by the following number of seconds	Specify the number of seconds to rewind from start of paragraph when playing audio and video.
Tuning Wizard	Click this button to verify that audio and/or video hardware is functioning properly.

Shared Session

The Shared Session options are shown in Figure A-23. The options are described in Table A-9.

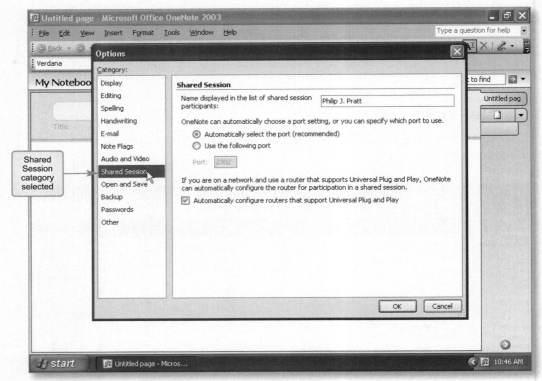

FIGURE A-23

Table A-9 Shared Session Options	
OPTION	**DESCRIPTION**
Name displayed in the list of shared session participants	Name that will be displayed during shared session.
Port setting	Select desired option button to have OneNote choose the port or to specify the port directly.
Automatically configure routers that support Universal Plus and Play	If checked, OneNote will configure such routers automatically. Otherwise it will not.

Backup

The Backup options are shown in Figure A-24. The options are described in Table A-10 on the next page.

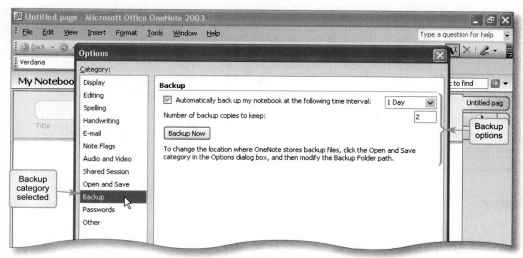

FIGURE A-24

Table A-10 Backup Options	
OPTION	**DESCRIPTION**
Automatically back up my notebook at the following time interval	Backup will occur at interval specified. Select an interval between 1 Minute and 6 Weeks.
Number of backup copies to keep	Specify the number of backup copies to keep.
Backup Now	Click this button to perform immediate backup.

Passwords

The Passwords options are shown in Figure A-25. The options are described in Table A-11.

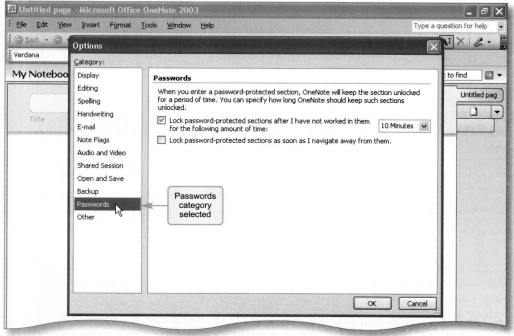

FIGURE A-25

Table A-11 Passwords Options

OPTION	DESCRIPTION
Lock password-protected sections after I have not worked in them for the following amount of time.	If checked, once the indicated amount of time has passed with no activity on the section, the section will be locked. Otherwise, it will not.
Lock password-protected sections as soon as I navigate away from them.	If checked, the section will be locked as soon as you navigate away from the section. Otherwise, it will not.

Other

The Other options are shown in Figure A-26. The options are described in Table A-12.

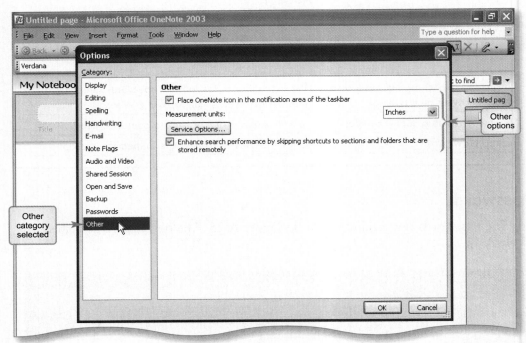

FIGURE A-26

Table A-12 Other Options

OPTION	DESCRIPTION
Place OneNote icon in notification area of the taskbar	If checked, OneNote icon will appear. Otherwise, it will not.
Measurement units	Select the unit of measure for your notes.
Service Options	Click to access special service options: Customer Feedback Options, Online Content, and Shared Workspace.
Enhance search performance by skipping shortcuts to sections and folders that are stored remotely	If checked, will enhance performance by skipping shortcuts.

Index

 # Quick Reference Summary

In Microsoft Office OneNote 2003, you can accomplish a task in a number of ways. The following table provides a quick reference to each task presented in this textbook. The first column identifies the task. The second column indicates the page number on which the task is discussed in the book. The subsequent four columns list the different ways the task in column one can be carried out. You can invoke the commands listed in the MOUSE, MENU BAR, and SHORTCUT MENU columns using Voice commands.

Microsoft Office OneNote 2003 Quick Reference Summary

TASK	PAGE NUMBER	MOUSE	MENU BAR	SHORTCUT MENU	KEYBOARD SHORTCUT
Backup, Perform Immediate	ONE 51		Tools | Options | Backup category | Backup Now button		
Bullet Style, Select	ONE 86	Bullets button on Formatting toolbar	Format | Bullets		
Bulleted List, Create	ONE 86	Bullets button on Formatting toolbar	Format | Bullets		CTRL+PERIOD (.)
Changes, Undo	ONE 21	Undo button on Standard toolbar	Edit | Undo		CTRL+Z
Characters, Format	ONE 24	Bold, Italic, or Underline button on Formatting toolbar	Format | Font		CTRL+B (bold), CTRL+I (italic), CTRL+U (underline)
Characters, Highlight	ONE 25	Pen button arrow on Standard or Drawing and Writing Tools toolbar, highlight selection or Highlight button on Formatting toolbar			
Container, Add	ONE 19	Click position for container			
Container, Delete	ONE 23	Delete button on Standard toolbar		Delete	DELETE
Container, Move	ONE 20	Drag container		Move	
Container, Resize	ONE 21			Resize	
Container, Split	ONE 23	Select portion to be moved, then drag			
Content, Copy	ONE 22	Copy button on Standard toolbar	Edit | Copy	Copy	CTRL+C
Content, Cut	ONE 22	Cut button on Standard toolbar	Edit | Cut	Cut	CTRL+X
Content, Paste	ONE 22	Paste button on Standard toolbar	Edit | Paste	Paste	CTRL+V
Deleted Page, Recover	ONE 77			Right-click tab for deleted page in Deleted Pages folder, then click Restore	
Drawing or Handwriting, Erase	ONE 43	Eraser button on Standard or Drawing and Writing Tools toolbar			

Microsoft Office OneNote 2003 Quick Reference Summary *(continued)*

TASK	PAGE NUMBER	MOUSE	MENU BAR	SHORTCUT MENU	KEYBOARD SHORTCUT
Drawing, Add	ONE 40	Pen button on Standard or Drawing and Writing Tools toolbar, Selection Tool button on Standard or Drawing and Writing Tools toolbar when done	Tools | Drawing and Writing Tools		
Extra Writing Space, Add	ONE 43	Insert Extra Writing Space button on Drawing and Writing Tools toolbar	Insert | Extra Writing Space	Extra Writing Space	
Folder, Add	ONE 69		File | New | Folder or Insert | New Folder	New Folder	
Folder, Delete	ONE 79		File | Current Folder | Delete	Delete	
Handwriting, Use	ONE 42	Pen button, on Standard or Drawing and Writing Tools toolbar Selection Tool button on Standard or Drawing and Writing Tools toolbar when done	Tools | Drawing and Writing Tools		
Note Flags Summary Page, Create	ONE 96	Create Summary Page button in Note Flags Summary task pane			
Note Flags Summary, View	ONE 94	Note Flags Summary button on Standard toolbar	View | Note Flags Summary		
Note Flags, Add	ONE 89	Note Flag button on Standard toolbar	Format | Note Flags	Note Flags	
Note Flags, Use	ONE 89	Note Flag button on Standard toolbar			
Notes, E-mail	ONE 130	E-mail button on Standard toolbar	File | Send To | Mail Recipient		CTRL+SHIFT+E
Numbered List, Create	ONE 87	Numbering button on Formatting toolbar	Format | Numbering		CTRL+/
Numbering Style, Select	ONE 87	Numbering button on Formatting toolbar	Format | Numbering		
Outline, Collapse	ONE 104		View | Hide Levels Below		ALT+SHIFT+level number
Outline, Create	ONE 30				Type a number, press TAB
Outline, Expand	ONE 105		View | Hide Levels Below		ALT+SHIFT+level number
Outline, Select Text at Same Level	ONE 105		Edit | Select, and then select level		
Page, Add	ONE 26	New Page button on Standard toolbar or New Page tab	File | New | New page or Insert | New Page	New Page	CTRL+N
Page, Add Title	ONE 27	Click title area, type title			
Page, Delete	ONE 77	Delete button on Standard toolbar		Delete	DELETE
Page, Move	ONE 75	Move Page To button on Standard toolbar	Edit | Move Page To	Move Page To	
Page, Rename	ONE 90	Click title area, type new title			
Pages, Group	ONE 78		Edit | Group Pages	Group Pages	
Pages, Ungroup	ONE 78		Edit | Ungroup Pages	Ungroup Pages	
Pen Color, Select	ONE 40	Pen button arrow			

Microsoft Office OneNote 2003 Quick Reference Summary

TASK	PAGE NUMBER	MOUSE	MENU BAR	SHORTCUT MENU	KEYBOARD SHORTCUT
Pen Type, Select	ONE 40	Pen button arrow on Standard or Drawing and Writing Tools toolbar			
Pictures, Add	ONE 37		Insert | Picture		
Playback Audio Notes from Specific Position	ONE 132	Audio flag for selected item in audio note container			
Playback Entire Audio Note	ONE 132	Play button on Audio Recording toolbar or Audio flag for audio note container			
Print All Pages in Section	ONE 47		File | Print | All option button		
Print Current Page	ONE 48	Print button on Standard toolbar	File | Print | Pages		
Quit OneNote	ONE 54	Close button on title bar	File | Exit		ALT+F4
Record Notes	ONE 132	Play button on Audio Recording toolbar			
Research Task Pane, Use	ONE 125	Research button on Standard toolbar	Tools | Research		
Rule Lines, Remove	ONE 50	Show/Hide Rule Lines button on Standard toolbar			
Rule Lines, Show	ONE 48	Show/Hide Rule Lines button on Standard toolbar	View | Rule Lines, select style		
Search Notes	ONE 91	Edit | Find		CTRL+F	
Section Color, Change	ONE 18		Format | Section Color	Section Color	
Section, Close	ONE 15		File | Current Section | Close	Close	CTRL+W
Section, Create	ONE 16	New Section button on Standard toolbar	File | New | Section or Insert | New Section	New Section	
Section, Delete	ONE 16		File | Current Section | Delete	Delete	
Section, Move	ONE 71			Move	
Section, Open	ONE 17		File | Open		CTRL+O
Section, Rename	ONE 16		File | Current Section | Rename	Rename	
Section, Save to Another Location	ONE 129		File | Save As		
Side Note, Create	ONE 97	OneNote icon in notification area on Windows taskbar	Window | New Side Note Window		CTRL+SHIFT+M
Spell Check	ONE 101		Tools | Spelling		F7
Stationery, Create Custom	ONE 82		File | New | Save current page as stationery link		
Stationery, Use	ONE 80		File | New | Change stationery area		
Subpage, Add	ONE 44		File | New | Subpage or Insert | New Subpage	New Subpage	

Microsoft Office OneNote 2003 Quick Reference Summary *(continued)*

TASK	PAGE NUMBER	MOUSE	MENU BAR	SHORTCUT MENU	KEYBOARD SHORTCUT
Switch to Selection Tool	ONE 42	Selection Tool button on Standard or Drawing and Writing Tools toolbar			
Symbols, Insert	ONE 24		Insert | Symbol		
Table, Add	ONE 46				Type text, press TAB, BACKSPACE, and ENTER
Task Pane, Close	ONE 9	Close button on task pane title bar	View | Task Pane		CTRL+F1
Text, Move	ONE 22	Select text, then drag			